THE STORYBOOK OF OPERA
Volume I

The dramas of: Die Fledermaus, Romeo et Juliette, The
Barber of Seville, Carmen, The Force of Destiny, La
Traviata, La Boheme, Madama Butterfly

by
Cyrus Henry Biscardi

Foreword by Franco Corelli

LP LEARNING PUBLICATIONS, INC.
Holmes Beach, Florida

Library of Congress Cataloging-in-Publication Data

Biscardi, Cyrus H. (Cyrus Henry)
   The Storybook of Opera, Volume I

   Includes bibliographies and indexes.
   Summary: Presents the stories of "Die Fledermaus,"
"Romeo et Juliette," "Carmen," and five other operas.
Also includes a list of American and international
opera companies and a glossary of operatic terms.
   1. Operas—Stories, plots, etc.—Juvenile literature.
2. Opera—Juvenile literature. [Operas—Stories,
plots, etc.   2. Opera]   I. Title
MT95.B   782.1'3   86-81155
ISBN 0-918452-93-7 (v. 1)
ISBN 1-55691-007-X (pbk. : v. 1)

Learning Publications, Inc.
PO Box 1326, 5351 Gulf Drive
Holmes Beach, Florida 34217-1326

Illustrations by Kitty Chang

Printing: 1 2 3 4 5 6 7 8 9   Year: 7 8 9 0 1 2

DEDICATION

To Franco Corelli, for the beauty, excitement and—above all—
that special emotion he brought into our lives.

CONTENTS

Volume I

Contents of Volume II, *The Storybook of Opera*:
    Tosca, L'Elisir d'Amore (The Elixir of Love), Tristan und Isolde, Rigoletto, Il Trovatore (The Troubadour), Die Zauberflote (The Magic Flute), and Hansel und Gretel. Foreword by Ann Blyth.

FOREWORD

When I first started to read the manuscript of this Storybook, I soon noticed how easy it was to follow the story and to understand the characters and the music. For the first time, these opera stories really come to life, and you get to know why opera has been such an important art form for so many years.

When you meet Romeo and Juliet, for example, you can see how they become so much in love that they long to be together even into the next world. I found it especially interesting that Charles Gounod and his librettists kept very close to Shakespeare's drama so that we get the best of the play set to beautiful music, with all the emotion and despair felt by these young lovers.

I like the way the stories flow from one to the other so that you find you are carried along throughout the entire book, rather than stopping after each one. For instance, from Carmen who is fatalistic and believes that she is governed by the forces of destiny, we go to the next story which is actually called *The Force of Destiny* (*La Forza del Destino*) where we see how circumstances beyond our control can shape our lives for better or for worse.

Even though I have spent a great part of my life close to the famous characters that you meet when you read this Storybook, I still found it fascinating to relive the trials and joys of Alfredo and his Violetta, Rodolfo and Mimi, and Cio-Cio-San and the faithless Pinkerton.

It is therefore, with particular pleasure, that I recommend to readers of all ages that they explore the world of opera as presented in this new and different Storybook—a book that will certainly help make opera an important experience in the lives of millions everywhere.

Franco Corelli

PREFACE

When I first thought about how best to present the stories of opera to readers of all ages, I recalled my own experience, and decided that short synopses, even libretto translations just do not fill the need for a dramatic, easy-to-read approach that *invites* the reader to explore the world of opera.

Having been introduced to this world at the age of six, it was not easy for me to understand what it was all about. I wanted to read these stories the way I was accustomed to reading stories, with dialogue and descriptions of the characters and the places where the action occurs. And that's what I hope *The Storybook of Opera* will do for you.

Since I knew how important it was to be careful in translations, I went over each opera word for word and note for note. However, if by translating the words as they are written, the meaning might not emerge as clearly as it should, the *true sense* of what is being said has been put down so that the story may be more easily understood. In this respect, not only newcomers but opera buffs of all ages will benefit.

I use ellipses (the three dots) and dashes throughout the two volumes that initiate this storybook so that you may get a sense of the *music* as well—the flow, rhythm and phrasing. Of course, ellipses are also needed to indicate that not *all* the words have been put down in a particular aria.

Finally, the enjoyment of opera rests with the singers you hear, whether at the opera house, home recordings or telecasts.

One famous artist who thrilled us as few have, is the star who has written the foreword to this volume. It is impossible to ever forget his dynamic stage presence and the depth of his acting, not to mention his uniquely beautiful quality of voice. Franco Dorelli's poignant Don Jose, his tender Romeo, his forceful Andrea Chenier (the poet who was caught up in the turmoil of the French Revolution), and so many other outstanding performances, will live in memory and in his everlasting recordings.

Similarly, it is indeed a pleasure to have a foreword to Volume II written by lovely Ann Blyth, a film star whose splendid lyric voice filled international theatres, and who extended her musical and dramatic gifts to the legitimate stage as well as to the television screen.

In conclusion, a word must be said about "operatic license." There are some opera plots that do stretch one's ability to understand. For example, in *The Force of Destiny* (*La Forza del Destino*) it is never explained how or why the lovers became separated (for years) after fleeing the wrath of the mortally wounded Marquis. We just have to believe that it *could* happen and let it go at that.

In sum, *Storybook* is a new way to enter and appreciate a most fascinating, fulfilling and emotional Wonderland.

ACKNOWLEDGEMENTS

Out of quite a few, there are some especially whom I would like to thank. The envelope please:

Marion and Don Rahman who introduced me to a certain important celebrity. Oscar Muller, overseer of what I translated from the German, and other things. John Castellana for witnessing the deed. Paul Zangas, artistic specifier. My brother Jeff, for his professional handling of the covers. My daughter Denise, for valuable young-person opinions. Kitty Chang for her "no problem" attitude. Roslyn's William Cullen Bryant Library staffers who found the references I needed. Edsel Erickson, Publisher, for his enthusiasm and warmth, and his most capable and understanding staff. And to Mrs. Corelli for her gracious help and thoughtfulness.

And through it all, the encouragement, the love, the resolve of my dear wife Dorothy who typed and retyped the manuscript until it seemed it would never end. Thanks.

Introduction

How many of you remember reading *Alice in Wonderland*? Remember how Alice wondered what it would be like if she could walk *Through the Looking Glass,* and what she would find on the other side? Suddenly the glass grew misty and soft, and as Alice stepped through she was in a marvelously new and different world.

Imagine how great it would be if you could do the same thing today. I think you can. Not walk through a mirror, but really step into an amazing world of beauty, love, intrigue, violence and emotion—filled with real people and "jabberwocky" ones. Characters that cry and laugh, who show us all of life's ups and downs—but do it in a way that's *grand,* lifting us up on waves of wonderful music and song.

In bringing you these stories I hope to show you that there

is nothing so mysterious about opera. The plots and the characters (and some of them *are* characters), though sometimes complicated, are really about the things that you and so many others feel almost every day, or read about in the daily newspapers, or see on television—with one big difference: they're combined with the musical genius of composers who were moved by the story to reach the tops in melody and drama.

And now, if you're ready to walk with me "through the looking glass," let's go to Lincoln Center in New York City.

We're standing in front of the Metropolitan Opera House, one of the many fabulous opera houses found almost everywhere in the world. The long, arched windows are all lit up and we see the colorful Chagall murals on each side. As we go inside everything becomes red and gold and marble. We walk up the circling staircase and onto the balcony called the Grand Tier.

Here we notice that right in front of us is a beautiful hanging chandelier that looks like a clustering burst of stars. There are twelve of these star-bursts hanging around the front of this balcony. Well, they're nice, but how are we going to see the stage with these "stars" in our eyes?

There's a surprise waiting for us. The audience settles down. The lights start to dim. (There are other lights, like diamonds, attached around all five balconies—plus side lights that look like bright marbles.) At this same moment, the hanging star-bursts slowly begin to float upward, higher and higher, until they join the one giant burst at the golden ceiling. Now everyone is smiling like Alice's Cheshire cat!

Now the only lights we see are those shining for the musicians and where the conductor will guide the orchestra. There's a little sound of clapping as he takes his place. He turns to the audience and bows. The wonderful moment has arrived when the music is about to begin.

And where will it take us? To Vienna, Austria! The Vienna of April 5, 1874 in the Theater an der Wien. That's where this light, gay, romantic and funny opera *Die Fledermaus* (Dee FLAY-der-mouse), by Johann Strauss, was first performed.

The original play, by Henri Meilhac and Ludovic Halevy, was called *Le Reveillon* (The Christmas Eve Party). But Maximilian Steiner, a director of the Viennese theater, had Richard Genee (one of his conductors) and writer Carl Haffner do the *libretto*. Strauss liked it so much that he wrote the music in *six weeks!*

You might think that *The Bat* is a mystery story. But in fact, it is such a happy opera that it has become traditional for New Year's Eve! And no wonder! It's full of champagne, beautiful women and handsome men dancing under brilliant crystal chandeliers to the marvelous tunes of Johann Strauss, the Waltz King.

To give you some idea of how Strauss had captured the world even before he composed *The Bat,* let's see what happened in Boston in the summer of 1872.

Strauss had been invited to conduct at the World's Peace Jubilee. He didn't like the idea of crossing the ocean, but he had been given an offer he couldn't refuse: a guarantee of one hundred thousand dollars, deposited to his account in a European bank. This would be a sizable sum even today. Just imagine what it was over a hundred years ago.

Well, Boston was a young city in a young country and nothing was too good for the young, handsome Johann whom the girls loved and the men envied. So, the Bostonians thought the orchestra should be big too. Would you believe that Strauss was to conduct over a thousand musicians: four hundred first violins, two hundred second violins, one hundred cellos, one hundred violas, one hundred basses, one hundred woodwinds and one hundred in the brass section? But it didn't stop there. The chorus numbered twenty thousand! Strauss had twenty assistant conductors who would signal his every move! Here's what he himself had to say about this typically American event:

"Now I was face to face with . . . one hundred thou-

sand Americans. There I stood at a raised desk, high above all the others. Suddenly a cannon shot rang out, a gentle hint for us twenty-thousand-odd to begin the Blue Danube. I gave the signal, my twenty assistant conductors followed as quickly and as well as they could, and there broke out an unholy row such as I shall never forget. As we had begun more or less together I concentrated. . .on seeing that we should finish together too! Thank Heaven, I managed even that! The hundred thousand mouths in the audience roared applause and I breathed a sigh of relief when I found myself in fresh air again and felt the solid ground under my feet."

What a night that must have been! Thousands wanting his autograph, a handshake, or just a smile.

In October of 1894, fifty years after his debut as a composer, there was a week-long celebration for him. Johann Strauss had taken music out of aristocratic halls and brought it to the people. The Emperor Franz Joseph was there. Strauss was deeply moved by this honor. "If it is true that I have talent," he said, "I owe it above everything else to my beloved city of Vienna. . .the city of beautiful women who inspire. . .the artist. Vienna is not indebted to me for what I have done. It is I who must eternally be indebted to Vienna for what she gave me."

Johann Strauss lived to be seventy-four. In Vienna, today, you can see a memorial to him. . .as he stands playing his violin. . . seeming to sway to the melodies of his famous waltzes. And today at the Met—with the star-bursts (a gift from Austria) darkened—we wait for the first notes of. . .

1

Die Fledermaus

(Dee FLAY-der-mouse)

All the tunes in the overture will be heard later in the opera, sung by the people we will soon meet. The first one may be Dr. Falke (FAHL-keh)—*The Bat* himself. He sometimes appears before the curtain goes up, although some productions tell the story through a conversation between the doctor and his friend Eisenstein in the first act.

To make things clear we'll begin with a...

PROLOGUE

Dr. Falke tells us that he is called Dr. Fledermaus because not long ago he and his friend, Eisenstein, were taking each other home from a fancy dress ball. His friend was dressed as a

butterfly and Falke as a bat. "On the way home," recalls Dr.
Falke, "I passed out in the carriage and my best friend left me
there asleep in the public square. In the morning I was awaken-
ed by a hundred people laughing at me!" Since then he is called
Dr. Fledermaus. So now he plans his revenge, and it will happen tonight. "Good Lord! Look at the time! I must fly! Er...I
mean *walk* to Eisenstein's now!"

ACT I

When the curtain goes up we are inside Gabriel von
Eisenstein's house. It is evening. The living room windows look
out on the garden. Off stage we hear the voice of Alfredo singing a serenade to Rosalinda. About four years ago they thought
they were meant for each other, but it never worked out—and
now she's married to Gabriel.

At about the same time, Adele, the maid, comes into the room.
She hears Alfredo but pays little attention. Her mind is taken
up with a letter in her hand. It's from her sister, inviting her
to a grand ball that evening. The ball will be at Prince Orlofsky's
palace and, of course, *everybody* will be there.

> "I surely would like to go to this marvelous ball. But how
> can I get away? I have work to do, and yet, maybe I can
> think of something."

Adele leaves somewhat sadly. At this moment Rosalinda appears hurriedly from her bedroom. She's adjusting her robe and
seems quite upset.

> "That Alfredo!" she says, "Can you imagine him
> serenading me when he knows that I'm married? But he
> does have a beautiful voice!"

Adele comes in sobbing, holding a picture of her aunt:

> "Madame, I have a sick aunt."

> "Well, go take a pill," says Rosalinda, absentmindedly.

> "No, not me, it's my aunt. This one. She's very sick."

"She looks healthy to me."

"She's so sick," repeats Adele.

"Then let *her* take a pill. I can't spare you Adele—especially since my husband has to go to jail for a week."

"Jail? What for?"

"For hitting a tax collector! I can't let you go."

Adele runs from the room, sobbing as she goes.

Alfredo comes bounding in from the garden.

"Alfredo!" cries Rosalinda, "You must leave!"

"That's not what I had in mind."

"But my husband will be here in a moment."

"Yes...but he'll soon be gone for a whole week."

"I'm not so sure about that. He's with his lawyer now."

"But you love me."

"No, not you...perhaps your voice."

Alfredo sings his serenade again and by the time he hits the top note Rosalinda has melted. Alfredo leaves her there and with a flourish disappears out the window.

Gabriel von Eisenstein and his lawyer, Dr. Blind, arrive. They are arguing about the case. It seems Dr. Blind didn't do so well when it came to keeping Eisenstein out of jail. In fact, instead of one week, he now has to serve *two!*

"Dr. Blind you are a nincompoop!" says Eisenstein in disgust. "The best thing you can do right now is leave. At once!"

Rosalinda comes to him.

"Oh, Gabriel...what am I going to do without you—for two whole weeks."

Adele enters with a calling card, and announces that Dr. Falke is here. Falke comes bustling in and goes to Rosalinda.

"Congratulations!" he exclaims with pleasure. "You'll be rid of *him* for two whole weeks! Ah, Gabriel, just think if your lawyer had kept on talking he could have gotten you a whole month!"

Rosalinda leaves the room and Dr. Falke takes the chance to tell Gabriel he should be happy about going to jail since it will be the perfect way to go to the ball.

"A ball? It seems I'll be going to jail instead."

"Not tonight! What's wrong with stopping off at Prince Orlofsky's first and reporting to jail in the morning? Think of the beautiful girls. In fact, there's one in particular I want you to meet. A Hungarian Countess! Tell me, do you have that fascinating little watch all the girls used to go crazy for?"

"Of course. Here it is. But it's just a memory now. I haven't used it in years. After all, I'm a happily married man."

"Hmmm...how many females were promised this chiming watch?" asks Falke.

"Eighty-six...no, eighty-seven."

"And not one of them got it? Not even Rosalinda?"

"Not one. Not even Rosalinda."

"Well, bring it along tonight—I think you'll have use for it!"

Eisenstein begins to brighten and before long both he and Dr. Falke are dancing around the living room. This is when Rosalinda comes back.

"Well! You certainly cheered him up in a hurry," she says, surprised.

"See you later!" Eisenstein tells her.

"What do you mean? I was going with you—wasn't I?"

"Oh, no...it would be too much. Fritz will introduce—I mean—take me. Mustn't be late!"

Eisenstein, with a new spring to his step, goes off quickly to his bedroom to dress for "jail."

Falke turns to Rosalinda.

"Now that Gabriel is forced to leave you alone...I have a suggestion. Why not come to Orlofsky's ball tonight? You could be masked and arrive as a mysterious Hungarian Countess."

"Why,...I don't know if I could..."

"Of course you can! See you later. Good night!"

Rosalinda is left in the room with a faraway look in her eyes. Adele enters.

"Adele, is your aunt still sick?"

"My aunt?"

"Yes, your *sick* aunt!"

"Oh-h-h-h...yes, very sick."

"Then take the night off and go see her."

"But..."

"Adele!"

"Yes, madame, thank you very much madame...I'll get dressed."

Before she leaves the room, Eisenstein appears grandly dressed in white tie and tails. Both women are flabbergasted.

"Well," he says. Eisenstein looks at them for a moment. "After all, just because I'm going to jail I can't forget that I'm a gentleman!"

"We'll miss you," Rosalinda says, not too convincingly.

She then sings a sorrowful, but beautiful song, telling him how much she'll miss him.

"Good-bye, my darling...," waves Eisenstein.

"Good-bye, madame...," says Adele as she leaves.

Rosalinda is left alone, but not for long. Alfredo has been waiting for just this moment and he comes in once again to try to interest Rosalinda. He knows that Rosalinda's weakness is his stirring, Italian tenor voice, so he plans to sing her a delightful little song. But first, he boldly goes into the bedroom and returns wearing Eisenstein's silk dressing robe! Rosalinda wants him to take it off. Since dinner is on the table he believes it only proper to wear this comfortable robe, he tells Rosalinda, and then bursts into song.

He's not quite finished when Rosalinda interrupts him.

"Be quiet! I hear a voice!"

"Of course you do...," says Alfredo with satisfaction.

"No, no...someone's coming. We're caught!"

After a few knocks on the door, Frank the Warden comes striding into the room. He looks like anything but a jailor since he too is dressed for the ball.

"Good evening. I am Frank the Warden and I'm here to escort your husband to jail."

Rosalinda starts to tell him that Alfredo is not her husband, but catches herself. Alfredo gives Frank a glass of champagne and, before we know it, all three are singing a lively trio. Frank is wondering what is going on. Alfredo is saying that he's certainly not going to jail. And Rosalinda is caught in the middle, trying to convince Alfredo he should protect her "honor" and go with Frank. Finally, the warden grabs Alfredo by the arm and starts to drag him off. Alfredo, clutching a bottle of champagne, begs one kiss from Rosalinda. She agrees, just to get rid of him. And, with all three singing brightly, Alfredo is carted off to jail.

ACT II

When the curtain opens, we find ourselves at the rich Prince Orlofsky's party. It's a gorgeous palace with liveried servants, winding staircases, lovely chandeliers and, of course, the beautiful people having a marvelous time. A chorus sings. The ladies are gossiping, and the men are too. Adele is there looking stunning in one of Rosalinda's gowns. Her sister, Ida, is there as well and they are both living high. In the center of it all is the handsome prince smoking a cigarette held in an enormous cigarette holder. Dr. Falke approaches and asks him how he is. "Bored," replies the Prince. In fact at most everything Falke suggests, Orlofsky answers that it is "so boring."

> *(Incidentally, the part of the Prince is most often played by a woman dressed as a man. She has a mezzo-soprano voice, which means that it is lower in tone than a regular soprano. This is one of those unusual things that happen in opera, but you soon get used to it and enjoy the beauty of this quality of voice. These parts are called "pants roles.")*

Trying to get himself out of his "boredom," Orlofsky asks Falke about some "special entertainment" that he, Falke, had mentioned to him. "Sh!" says Falke, telling the Prince that he will be very amused by the little drama that will be played. He's referring, of course, to his revenge on Eisenstein.

About this time, Adele wants to be introduced to the Prince. Ida would rather not. Adele says, "All right, I'll introduce myself!"

> "No, wait," Ida replies, quickly. "Excellency, this is my sister...er..."

> "Olga," prompts Adele.

> "Olga," repeats Ida.

> "And how are you enjoying yourself, Miss Olga?"

> "Boring."

The Prince laughs and gives them both a lot of gold coins so they can enjoy themselves at the gambling tables.

When they leave, Falke tells the Prince that Olga is not Olga but Adele, his "hero's" *chambermaid!* "She's one of my characters in *"The Bat's Revenge,"* he explains. At the top of the staircase a servant appears announcing "Monsieur, Le Marquis de Renard!" Falke quickly tells Orlofsky that this is his hero in tonight's play, and that he's no more a Marquis than Olga is Olga. He introduces Eisenstein to the Prince.

"I trust you will have a good time at my party, Marquis."

"I'm sure I will."

"My motto here is 'Chacun a son gout' (Shah-kun ah sone goo). Everyone does as he pleases."

With that, Orlofsky sings a catchy tune telling everyone of his philosophy, "Chacun a son gout." And so the party goes on its merry way with everybody laughing and loving and drinking and dancing.

In the middle of it all, Adele and Ida enter from the gaming room, having lost all the money the Prince gave them. Eisenstein spots Adele at once. It's his chambermaid! And that's his wife's dress she's wearing. Some nerve! Of course Adele has spotted her boss and wonders what he's doing here when he's sup posed to be in jail! She asks Ida nervously, "What do I do?" "Well," says Ida, "you've always wanted to be an actress— here's your chance!"

Meanwhile, Eisenstein is thinking that if he recognizes Adele, she surely is going to recognize *him*. Anyway, they meet, introduced by the Prince who is beginning to think that maybe this whole thing will really be fun after all.

"Why are you staring at me, my dear Marquis?" asks Adele.

"It's amazing, Miss Olga, but you look exactly like my chambermaid."

"How dare you?"

"Don't take offense. This chambermaid of mine is a beauty, a wonder," says Eisenstein.

He takes another glass of champagne. He's been drinking ever since he arrived and by now is feeling very light-hearted.

Adele sings a light, bright song telling everyone to just look at her "elegant grace" and they can see at once that she is a lady and not a lady's maid! She's full of laughter at *that* silly idea!

From the head of the staircase a servant announces another guest. It's Frank the Warden! "Monsieur, le Duc de Bastille!" At this, Prince Orlofsky tells Dr. Falke that he is really beginning to enjoy the comedy. "Wait till my leading lady arrives," laughs Falke, "then the fun will really begin!"

"Countess Halandza!" announces the servant.

Dr. Falke quickly goes to the "Hungarian Countess" who is beautifully dressed and is holding a sparkling half-mask before her eyes.

"But my husband will recognize me," pouts Rosalinda.

"Not at all," says Falke, "he's seeing everything through a cloud of champagne bubbles!"

"Good heavens!" exclaims Rosalinda, as she sees her husband. "He's going through that chiming watch routine with our maid!"

Adele brushes off Eisenstein and runs away. This gives Falke his chance.

"She's here," he tells Eisenstein.

"Who?"

"The Countess."

"What countess?"

"The one I told you about...full of fire, Hungarian blood—goulash—and all that sort of thing."

"Do you think she'd like to know what time it is?" says Eisenstein slyly, holding up his little watch.

"Why not ask her?"

Eisenstein stumbles over to Rosalinda and starts to flirt with her. He tells her that she reminds him of his wife, but the Countess' hair is a much brighter red!

"What a lovely watch," she says.

Well, this is all that Eisenstein needs. From this point on it's a "duel" between the two. He's trying to woo his own wife and she's getting madder and madder at his flirting. As their duet's melody gets brighter and brighter, Rosalinda snatches the watch from her husband. Ignoring his pleading, she drops it down the front of her gown. Soon the Prince, Falke and other guests come in. Some of them ask the "Countess" to remove her mask. Others whisper that she probably is not Hungarian at all. With that, Rosalinda, alias Countess Halandza, gets the orchestra playing. She sings a *czardas*. She is sensational!

> "You are devastating!" exclaims Eisenstein. "Will you be my companion this evening? There's not much time—I have to be at—er—a—secret place at six."

He glances over at the warden, Frank, who is flirting with Adele.

> "But what about your wife?" asks Rosalinda, with a certain tone in her voice.

> "Oh, compared to you, she's a witch."

> "And compared to you, my dear Marquis, my husband is a liar and a cheat!"

Prince Orlofsky now takes center stage, raises his glass and offers a toast to champagne—the King of all Wines! Everyone sings. As this wonderful chorus comes to an end, Falke sings a toast saying that everyone should make the most of happiness, to have all the best that life can give...and the guests join in softly:

> "Happiness, here's to health and happiness...May it always be so."

The scene, like the song, is soft and a little sad. But the Prince calls out: "A waltz, let's have a waltz!" Everyone sings, as they dance to this delightful waltz...gowns swaying, lights glittering and Rosalinda still teasing her champagned husband. Suddenly the clock strikes! (Even these clock chimes have been played before in the overture to the opera.) Frank the Warden and Eisenstein stop in their tracks. "One, two, three, four, five, six..." Six in the morning! They're supposed to be at the jail!

All the guests watch and sing along as Frank and Gabriel Eisenstein leave arm in arm, waltzing as they go out into the early morning sun.

ACT III

Here we are, looking at the inside of the Municipal Jail. In the center is a large tea-making (or coffee) machine. And over in a corner near the door is Frosch, the jailor. He's been celebrating all by himself and by now is feeling very happy. Meanwhile, Alfredo (alias Eisenstein) has been singing at the top of his voice.

"Qui-ett!" shouts Frosch.

"I want a lawyer!" demands Alfredo.

The door opens and in weaves Frank the Warden. He takes off his hat and coat and has all he can do to finally find his desk chair.

> *(Now, you need to understand that this opera not only has been translated with different words, but has been performed under many different names: "Rosalinda," "The Merry Countess," "A Wonderful Night," "Champagne Sec," "The Masked Ball," "Fly-By-Night" and so on. Great liberties have also been taken with the character of Frosch, so you'll find him making jokes that are "of today.")*

Anyway, before long there's a knock on the door and in walk Adele and Ida. Adele wants Frank to live up to his promise of getting her into show business. And to show him how talented she is, she sings an *aria*. There's a kind of a marching tempo at one point and Frosch joins in behind her!

Another knock at the door. Frank quickly asks Frosch to hide the girls. In comes Eisenstein, humming the tune that Adele sang at the ball.

"What are *you* doing here, Frank?"

"What are *you* doing here, Gabriel?"

Frank now tells his friend that he's really the Warden. At the same time Eisenstein confesses that he really is Gabriel von Eisenstein and not a Marquis at all.

"What do you mean *you're* Eisenstein. . .I've got Eisenstein locked up in cell Number 12! He's been there all night."

"Can't be," says Eisenstein.

"I picked him up myself!"

"Where?"

"In his apartment. . .he was in his dressing gown with his wife. Embarrassing moment."

"His *dressing gown!*"

About this time Dr. Blind, the lawyer, arrives complete with wig, glasses, robe, and papers. He goes to Eisenstein.

"You sent for me?"

"No he didn't," says Frosch, "Mr. Eisenstein sent for you."

"But this *is* Mr. Eisenstein!"

"Well, there's two of them and the one upstairs sent for you."

"Just a minute," says Eisenstein, "let me have your wig, glasses and robe."

So over the objections of Dr. Blind, Gabriel begins to take his place. At that moment there's yet another knock on the door, so Eisenstein drags Dr. Blind off to complete his disguise. In walks Rosalinda, heavily veiled. Alfredo enters, still in the dressing gown. Frank and Frosch go out to the next room to find the real Eisenstein and the lawyer.

"Rosalinda," says Alfredo, "you didn't forget me!"

"No, of course not. I came to get you out before my husband arrives."

"Good. I've sent for a lawyer."

In comes Eisenstein in full disguise! Now there is a good deal of accusation back and forth. The climax arrives when Rosalinda (still angry at her husband for flirting at the ball) tells the "lawyer" that her husband is a monster!

"Aha," cries Eisenstein, "I am he!"

Off come the wig and glasses. Not to be outdone, Rosalinda triumphantly takes his watch from its hiding place. Now everyone is explaining to everyone. Adele and Ida have joined the mess. Frank is trying to patch things up.

Into all of this music and song enters Prince Orlofsky with his guests. The jail is transformed into a happy place full of color and sound.

"Here's to champagne—the King of all Wines!" exclaims the Prince again.

Everyone joins in to sing the same rousing chorus. The orchestra swells, the voices rise, as we see Gabriel and Rosalinda together again, while Dr. Falke, Alfredo, Adele, Frank, Ida and the whole company raise their glasses high.

THE CURTAIN FALLS

But all is not over. The opera house is filled with joyous applause just as it was at the Metropolitan premier of February 16, 1905! (Then, during Orlofsky's ball, twenty-nine world-famous artists joined in—including Enrico Caruso, Emma Eames and Antonio Scotti!) We see a bit of the curtain, at center stage, part. And out come the stars, one at a time, then all together. Curtain call follows curtain call. Gradually, the lights begin to brighten. Regretfully, we know the performance is over. Still the amusing story of Rosalinda and Gabriel lingers on in memory—but above all we take away with us the beautiful swaying waltz music of the immortal Johann Strauss.

And so we leave the Vienna of 1874, the gayest of all European cities, and head south to the sun and warmth of Italy. Twisting and turning through the snow-capped mountains, with postcard scenery on all sides, we travel backwards in time down to the medieval city of Verona. It is the 14th century.

The main square, or piazza, of the city is called the Piazza Bra, dominated by a fine marble Roman coliseum. People stroll along looking at the shops and at each other, and they gossip. We hear the latest about the well-known feuding families of Verona—the Montagues and the Capulets. A young man of the House of Montague has dared to crash a masked ball held at the palace of the Capulets! A young girl's name is also mentioned—a Capulet. These two teenagers have met and have fallen in love at first sight! It is the beginning of the story about the most famous lovers the world has ever known.

We softly sneak away. And slowly we leave our imagination to return to the 20th century and the opera house, where a performance of Charles Francois Gounod's lyrical work *Romeo and Juliet* is about to begin.

2

Romeo et Juliette

"For never was a story of more woe,
Than this of Juliet and her Romeo"

With these few words William Shakespeare sums up his immortal play. (Over ninety operas have been inspired by the plays of Shakespeare—close to twenty-five of them are about his two "star-crost lovers.") The most beautiful, "a perpetual love duet," is the one we are soon to see.

When Gounod began thinking about composing *Romeo et Juliette* in 1865, he fortunately called on two librettists, Jules Barnier and Michel Carre, who kept close to the original story so that today we have the best of Shakespeare and the best of the great French composer. Charles Gounod even begins with the Prologue, which gives you the strange feeling that the opera is starting at the *end!*

PROLOGUE

Lying side by side, together in death as they wished to be in life, Romeo and Juliet are mourned by their two families. There is a short, stormy overture by the orchestra setting the sad mood and then the chorus tells us of the feud of the rival families—how the young lovers paid with their lives in ending the hundred-year-old hatred. Soon, too, we hear the love theme, which will come back again and again as the story is told. The curtain closes on the dark and gloomy crypt.

ACT I

When the curtain rises again we are at a ball. Trumpets open with a fanfare. The guests are enjoying themselves in their masks and costumes—all lords and ladies waltzing around the brilliant-ly lit gallery. They tell of living life to the fullest...to grasp life before time rushes by never to return. The men tell of love and the inviting smiles and glances...as they look at the girls here and there. The women tell of how the men follow them, flirt with them, as they too remember how fast time flies.

On one side we hear Tybalt (Juliet's young cousin) asking Paris (the young lord who expects to marry Juliet) how he likes the party. "Wealth and beauty are the true guests," comments Paris.

"Don't you see the unique and priceless treasure that's destined to make you happy?" asks Tybalt. "Look!" he continues, "here she comes with her father."

The beautiful Juliet (who is only fourteen) enters, led by her father. The guests take away their masks in joyous anticipation.

"Welcome to my house," announces Capulet, "on this fami-ly occasion! This is my Juliet!"

All the ladies and gentlemen comment on how lovely she is, as a dance tune begins. Juliet is thrilled by everything. She loves

being the center of attraction. She is like a bird ready to fly. Her
father invites everyone to continue having a good time, to forget
any kill-joys, to greet youth and make way for the dancers! They
all gradually leave to stroll around in the nearby halls and rooms.
Juliet leaves too, escorted by Paris, as her father and Tybalt
follow.

It's here that Romeo comes in with his friends Mercutio,
(Mehr-KOO-shee-oh) Benvoglio (Ben-VOL-yo) and others.

"We're alone at last," says Mercutio. "Let's take off our
masks."

"No, not now!" warns Romeo. "You promised! Let's leave
before they recognize me."

Mercutio brags that he'll take care of any Capulet with his quick
sword. But Romeo has his doubts about the whole thing, even
whether they should have come at all.

"But why?" asks Mercutio, impatiently.

"I had a dream," Romeo replies.

Mercutio acts comically, as if he's terribly afraid.

"Oh, that's bad!" he says with mock horror, "Queen Mab
has visited you!"

"What?" asks Romeo, startled.

Mercutio tells of Mab, the Queen of Illusions, who presides
over dreams and is more fickle than the wind.

"Her chariot is made of an empty nutshell...her coachman
is a gnat...she lightly touches your lips and makes you
dream of kisses...!"

Romeo is not impressed and is still worried about being in
Capulet's home. Mercutio comments that Romeo is sad only
because his schoolboy crush, Rosaline, is not there. Before
Romeo has a chance to answer, he sees Juliet about to come
in with her nurse Gertrude. It is really love at first sight! Romeo
is struck by "This heavenly beauty who seems like a sunbeam
in the night!" And as he follows Juliet with his eyes he wonders,

"Did I love till now? Did I love?"

At this Mercutio and the others laugh.

"Good!" says Mercutio. "So to the devil with Rosaline!"

All of Romeo's young friends expected the breakup with Rosaline. Mercutio caps it all by declaring, "She's been dismissed...and so the comedy comes to an end!"

They hurry away as Juliet and Gertrude enter. Gertrude is saying that Juliet will have a "pearl" of a husband in Count Paris. But Juliet, although marriage has entered her mind, wants to remain free.

"Leave my heart to its springtime!"

She sings a cheery, carefree song. She wants to stay young.

"I want to live...this intoxication of youth lasts only a day!"

One of the Capulet's servants, Gregorio, meets Romeo. He's still masked and wants to know the name of "that fair child." But Gregorio misunderstands and replies that she is Gertrude. When Gertrude hears her name she turns and Gregorio tells her that she is needed to take care of supper. She and Gregorio leave. Romeo (hopefully) asks Juliet not to go.

Now follows a pretty *madrigal* for both voices, in which Romeo shyly begins to make love to Juliet. He kisses her hand. Their playful love-making no sooner ends than Romeo sees someone coming and quickly puts his mask on again.

"It's my cousin Tybalt," says Juliet.

Romeo suddenly realizes who Juliet really is! She must return to the ball or her friends will wonder. Then Tybalt suspiciously asks in a low voice about the young man who so quickly put on his mask. Juliet, of course, doesn't really know. But as they leave, Romeo makes the mistake of politely stepping aside and saying, "God keep you, sir." Tybalt instantly recognizes his voice! When Tybalt mentions his name Juliet is terrified. Romeo! Tybalt storms out swearing he will kill Romeo for daring to enter his house. Juliet is left standing all alone.

"Ah," she says... "Hatred is the cradle of this fatal love! It is ended! If I may not be Romeo's wife, let the grave be my wedding bed!"

She slowly leaves. Some of the guests enter. On one side Tybalt is with Paris, and on the other, Romeo, Mercutio, Benvoglio and their friends. Tybalt again sees Romeo! Paris asks him what he is so excited about. Tybalt points to Romeo.

"For this mortal insult, Romeo, I swear, shall suffer punishment!"

Meanwhile Romeo realizes the sadness of his love.

"My very name is a crime in her eyes!"

But Mercutio finds other things to worry about. He notices the black looks that Tybalt is throwing their way and he warns everyone to be quiet. Juliet's father asks all his guests to stay to drink and dance.

A ballet appears. As it ends the guests again start to joyfully dance to the same music as in the beginning of the act. Mercutio hurries Romeo out as Benvoglio and all their friends follow them into the night. The curtain falls.

ACT II

The violins softly play the plaintive love theme. The famous balcony scene is about to begin. Romeo, with the help of Stephano (STEH-fah-noh), his page, silently enters Juliet's garden. In the distance we hear Mercutio calling for him. To himself Romeo remarks that Mercutio has never felt the pangs of love.

"He jests at scars, (he) that never felt a wound!"

Romeo's friends, in chorus, sing that Romeo does not hear them, "May love guide his steps!" The voices fade away.

Romeo thinks of how much in love he is with Juliet. He begs the sun to rise so that he may see his Juliet once more. Suddenly a light appears in her window. In another moment Juliet is on the balcony. She is very sad. How can she hate Romeo? Romeo; why is he named Romeo? ("Romeo, wherefore art thou Romeo? Refuse that fatal name...")

Romeo hears her. He comes out of the shadows happy that Juliet returns his love.

"Is it true? Did you say it?"

"Who listens to me and surprises my secrets in the darkness of night?...Are you not Romeo?"

"No! I'll no longer be he if this detested name keeps us apart! That I may love you, let me born again...."

"Ah!...you know that the night hides my face from you...if your eyes could see its blushes...Dear Romeo! Tell me honestly 'I love you' and I'll believe you, and my honor will entrust itself to yours...as you can trust in me!"

"Before God who hears me, I pledge you my troth!"

Juliet hears someone coming! Romeo hides. It is Gregorio and the servants searching for intruders. But they find no one.

They tell Gertrude, who has just entered the garden, that they are hunting Montagues. If any Montagues dare to come back she'll take care of them! "We believe you!" Gregorio answers with a laugh. They say goodnight and leave.

When Juliet appears at the doorway, Gertrude asks her why she is not yet in bed.

"I was waiting for you!"

"Come in!"

"Don't scold!" whispers Juliet.

She takes one last look for Romeo and then goes into the house. Romeo is overjoyed.

"I fear to awaken and still dare not believe in its reality!"

Juliet can't stay away.

"Romeo!"

"Sweet love!"

He starts toward her, but she holds up her hand to stop him.

"One word only," she says, "then farewell! Tomorrow someone will come to find you."

Then sweetly solemn, as only a fourteen year old can be, she tells him,

"Upon your soul, if you want me as your wife send word to me what day, at what hour, in what place our union may be blessed in the sight of God! Then. . . to you will I yield up my whole life. . . and I'll renounce all that is not you! But if all your love intends is to trifle with me. . . then I beg you. . . see me no more and leave me to the grief which will fill my days."

Romeo kneels before her.

". . . I have told you I adore you. . . ."

Gertrude calls to Juliet from inside. Romeo rises and takes her hand.

"I'm coming," answers Juliet.

Romeo takes her in his arms as he tells her that no one is calling her.

"Let my hand forget itself in yours!"

"Someone might surprise us!"

Then together they sing some of the most famous love-words in all literature.

"Goodnight. . . Goodnight. . . parting is such sweet sorrow,"

as their voices soar into the night,

"that I would say goodnight till it be morrow. . . !
A thousand times goodnight," whispers Juliet.

She slips out of his arms and returns to her bed-chamber. Romeo watches her leave, longingly. Then, once again alone, he sings a flowing melody that's almost like a blessing.

"Go...rest peacefully...slumber...May a child's smile come gently to rest on your ruby lips! And...still whispering 'I love you' into your ear...may the night breeze bring you this kiss!"

And as the violins rise and fade with unbelievable sweetness, Romeo reluctantly leaves his Juliet as the curtain slowly falls.

ACT III

When the curtain rises we are in the monastery where Friar Laurence lives. The violins lead the music that sets the mood for what is about to happen. The Friar doesn't know it yet but he will soon be marrying his young friends. Romeo enters hurriedly.

"Father! God keep you!"

Friar Laurence is startled to see Romeo at such an early hour.

"What lover's care brings you?"

"You have guessed right, Father...it is love!"

"Love! Still the unworthy Rosaline...?"

Romeo scornfully rejects that idea saying at last, "Does one love Rosaline, having seen Juliet?"

Before the Friar can get over his surprise, Juliet arrives with Gertrude.

"Father," she says quickly, "this is my bridegroom... unite us before Heaven!"

The Friar, of course, agrees to help them, really hoping that by doing so the terrible feud will end. He begins the ceremony at once. Gertrude is keeping watch, ready to warn them of any danger. After the Friar prays to God to look favorably upon the union of the two young people before him he asks,

"Romeo, do you take Juliet as your wife?"

"Yes, Father!"

Then turning to Juliet, the Friar asks,

"Do you take Romeo for your husband?"

"Yes, Father!"

Now they exchange rings. Then, as Friar Laurence places Juliet's hand in Romeo's, he unites them in holy matrimony.

With that the young lovers joyfully sing of their union and their love. But now, alas, they must part...and Juliet leaves with Gertrude while Romeo stays with Friar Laurence as the music ends.

It is the end of scene one, act three. The next scene takes us to a street in Verona. The House of the Capulets is on the left.

Stephano is alone. (To achieve a light, youthful voice, this part of a young boy is played by a lyric soprano. It is another example of the so-called "pants role" in opera—a girl taking the part of a boy.) Stephano pretends to strum on his sword like a guitar as he sings about the "fair lady" of the Capulets surrounded by birds of prey. He goes on to warn that they had better guard her well as she will be drawn by love from their midst.

He soon gets the expected result. Gregorio appears, then the servants.

"Isn't this the fellow we chased away yesterday, dagger in hand?"

"The very one! He is very bold!"

Stephano hears them but continues his teasing song.

"Is it to flout us, my young friend, that you entertain us with this serenade?" asks Gregorio.

"I love music," Stephano replies.

"It's clear...you've had your guitar smashed...."

"For a guitar I have my sword and I know how to play more than one tune upon it."

"Ah, by God, for this kind of music we can give you a reply!''

Stephano, quickly drawing his sword all the way, replies, ''Then come and take a lesson from it!''

They begin to duel. The servants laugh.

''...he fights like a soldier...''

On this scene enter Mercutio and Benvoglio. Mercutio instantly steps between them with drawn sword.

"To set upon a boy...'tis a shameful deed worthy of Capulets!''

At the same moment, Tybalt arrives with Paris and friends.

''You have a ready tongue sir!''

''Not so ready as my arm,'' threatens Mercutio.

They start to duel! They have just about crossed their swords a half dozen times when Romeo rushes between them. This is what Tybalt really wants!

''Come on vile Montague...you are nothing but a coward!''

There is a moment of suspense, (the violins play a low and threatening strain). Romeo's hand swiftly draws his sword a short distance, but then he taps it back in place.

''Come now...Tybalt...I have reasons that disarm me...I am no coward! Farewell!''

Mercutio can't stand this.

''Romeo...did I hear you right? Very well then...the honor belongs to me!''

Romeo pleads with Mercutio, but his mind is made up. Tybalt and Mercutio now start to fight again. The friends on both sides mock each other, while Romeo sadly regrets the revengeful duel. Here the orchestra takes on a somewhat marching beat. We hear the trumpets and drums.

Then, at the height of the battle, Romeo once more tries to

stop the fight. And it is this very action that causes Tybalt to strike a death-blow! Mercutio is down! He looks at them all and speaks Shakespeare's familiar words: "A plague on both your houses." Then turning to Romeo he sadly asks, "Why came you between us?"

Tenderly his friends pick up the wounded Mercutio and carry him away. Romeo looks desperately after them, realizing that Mercutio is already dead. He no longer can control his rage. He draws his sword and cries, "...fury be my conduct now...Tybalt—there's no other coward here but you!" In less than a moment Romeo has struck down his enemy.

Capulet enters and runs to Tybalt's side to hold him. Benvoglio warns Romeo that Tybalt's wound is mortal and that he, Romeo, should escape at once. But Romeo only says to himself, "What have I done...I—to flee—cursed by *her!*"

By now the street is filled with townspeople. When they see that Tybalt is dead they all sing a funeral-like chorus as the orchestra, led by the violins, cries with them.

But soon the trumpets strike a fanfare and the Duke of Verona enters with his gentlemen and pages. Capulet begs him for justice.

"It's Tybalt, my nephew, slain by Romeo!"

"I avenged my friend, let my fate take its course!" replies Romeo.

Both sides plead for justice!

The Duke is angry at this constant fighting between these two families. He tells Romeo that according to law he should be put to death but since he did not start the fight, he is to be exiled! To the others he commands that they swear to obey his laws and the laws of God!

Realizing his fate, Romeo expresses his sorrow in a beautiful *aria* that rises and falls with his emotions, as he sees the end of "all the hopes and desires of my heart!"

All continue to be sorry for the terrible things that have happened. They agree to follow the Duke's law.

"Our hearts midst the blood and the tears will not forget their duty and their honor!"

The Duke once again turns to Romeo. He must leave the city by nightfall. In an outburst of despair Romeo sings, "I shall die...but I will see her again!"—as his voice soars thrillingly into the stratosphere. And with the chorus and orchestra swelling to a crashing climax (while Capulet insists there never will be peace), the curtain falls.

ACT IV

It is the newlyweds' wedding night. Juliet's bedroom is in semi-darkness for soon the dawn will arrive. The opening strains of the orchestra set the mood, telling of the deep love these two young people have for each other.

Juliet is the first to speak. She forgives Romeo for the death of Tybalt. After all, Tybalt hated Romeo and would have killed him! She tells her husband how much she loves him. Both sing of their "sweet night of love" in a passionate duet.

Suddenly Juliet asks, "What is it, Romeo?" And Romeo, rising quietly, bids her to listen to the song of the lark that tells them it is already the arrival of a new day.

But Juliet protests! She sings a lovely bittersweet aria, "No...no, it is not the day...it is not the lark...it is only the gentle nightingale...." Yet Romeo knows too well that it is truly "the dawn...breaking...in the mists of the East." The young bride still cannot accept the truth and pleads with him not to go. And so Romeo agrees! He will stay with her despite the mortal danger!

Juliet immediately realizes that he is right! She quickly tells him to leave her at once. But now Romeo takes up the same melody that Juliet had sung only moments before... "No...no, it is not the day. . . .'' The frightened Juliet insists and so Romeo sadly asks for one last kiss. . .asks her to remain just awhile longer in his arms.

The music now takes on a hurried tone—Juliet tells him once again that he must go. How cruel it is that they are forced to part forever! They reach a blend of voices that swells at the thought of ''tearing themselves away from each other. . . .''

Finally Romeo sings, ''Farewell, my Juliet!'' as they both pledge they will be forever true!

At last he leaves her. Juliet is now alone. And after a long musical pause she softly sings,

> ''Farewell. . .my life. . .heavenly angels, to you I entrust him. . .!''

The beautiful scene comes to a close.

In moments, with the trumpets sounding alarm and excitement, Gertrude enters. She sees with relief that Romeo has already gone, for here comes Juliet's father! Gertrude assures Juliet that he knows nothing about her marriage. She has no sooner said this than Capulet enters with Friar Laurence. Her father tells her that she must smile in spite of the death of Tybalt and that she will feel better by granting her cousin's last wish, which is to marry Paris! Juliet is greatly alarmed at this but the Friar whispers to her to be calm. Her father goes out to receive Paris and other friends, leaving the Friar and Juliet alone.

Juliet turns to him excitedly and tells him she is bewildered and afraid.

> ''It is for you to help me. . .for you to rescue me from my miserable fate! Speak, Father, or else I am ready to die!''

> ''So you are not afraid of death,'' notes Friar Laurence.

> ''Then drink this potion,'' he tells her, ''and suddenly your eyes will close as though in death.''

He goes on to explain, in almost a monotone, that the next day she will awaken and then she and her husband will be together again forevermore!

Without hesitating Juliet takes the vial, as Friar Laurence leaves..."till tomorrow...." The curtain falls.

When it rises again we hear organ music coming from the chapel. There is Juliet, Paris and her father, along with others in the wedding party. Paris comes forward to place a wedding band on Juliet's finger! But the potion has already begun to work. Suddenly, Juliet staggers as she cries, "Is this death? I am afraid! Father! Farewell!"

She falls senseless. Her father holds her, calls to her, but Juliet is "dead." All sing a dirge-like refrain. The orchestra, full and powerful, with kettle drums beating, swells...then softly subsides as this mournful scene comes to a gentle close.

ACT V

Once again we are in the crypt that opened the opera. A light, sad melody plays over the scene. Then the music hurries and reaches a height with trumpets blaring as Romeo appears. He is looking for Juliet.

We soon realize that somehow Friar Laurence's message, telling Romeo about the magic potion, never reached him. He is desperate at seeing his beautiful bride dead. He wishes only to be with her again...and so he bends down to clasp her once more in his arms, giving her one last kiss. The orchestra joins him in a lofty climax of sound. He then takes a poison flask from his doublet, drinks it down and throws it away.

"To you, my Juliet!"

Now the final ironic tragedy begins. Juliet stirs. "Where am I," she whispers. Romeo can't believe his eyes. Is this a dream? Do his fingers feel the warmth of her hand? Juliet turns and sighs at the sight of her beloved, "Romeo!"

Juliet is alive! Romeo is full of happiness.

"It is I. It is your husband!"

He folds her in his arms.

"Come, let us fly from here!"

But alas, it is too late.

Suddenly, Romeo begins to feel the pangs. The poison is taking its toll. Juliet is bewildered. Romeo painfully explains that since he believed his bride to be dead, he drank poison. Juliet cannot stand to hear this. But Romeo, in a tender melody, begs her to console herself with the thought that love is eternal. . .and will survive even the grave.

But Juliet cannot be consoled. Romeo, in a weakened voice, remembers back to when they were blissfully happy. Softly, the love music accompanies him as he sings once again the flowing phrase, "No. . .no it is not the day. . . . it is not the lark. . .it is the gentle nightingale, love's friend!" With that he slowly slips from her arms.

She quickly searches and finds the poison flask—but it is empty.

"Cruel husband," she cries, "you have not left me my share. . . ."

She remembers the dagger she had hidden in her dress and in a swift motion she stabs herself! Romeo half rises. Juliet falls into his arms with the words, "Ah! This moment is sweet," sung in a high, delicate voice. The violins set up a fearful, trembling sound; the orchestra takes up the familiar and woeful love theme and then fades into nothingness. Both ask the Lord to forgive them as with four final, thundering chords—the fateful story of Juliet and her Romeo comes to an end.

THE CURTAIN FALLS

For over 100 years this beautiful opera has been heard all over the world. It was in April, 1867 that it was first performed at the Theatre Lyrique in Paris. And, although it played at many opera houses from that moment on, it was not until 1888 that it finally arrived at the Paris Opera. For the first time the "ideal Romeo," the legendary Jean de Reszke, sang the part opposite the equally legendary girl from New Orleans, Adelina Patti.

Since most tenors are not born to look like the most famous of all young lovers, casting an ideal Romeo is not easy. However, in 1967 at the Metropolitan, there appeared on stage "the most handsome Romeo since Jean de Reszke," according to Harold Schonberg, noted critic of the *New York Times*. That night Franco Corelli joined the other few legendary Romeos that could sing and—most important—*look* the part of the young lover of Shakespeare's immortal play.

Charles Gounod, the composer of this lovely lyric opera, decided he wanted to write music from the time he was a very young boy. But under pressure from his mother, he went ahead and got a good general education. Still the music inside of him had to be born. Finally, at the age of eighteen, he was accepted to the Paris Conservatory. At twenty-one, he at last won the important Prix de Rome (just as did another Frenchman, Georges Bizet, as we shall soon see).

It was in Rome that Italian church music became his first love. At twenty-three, he had already written two Masses. He became so religious that he was seriously thinking of becoming a priest! However, music won out and before long his wonderful lyric talent was realized in the composing of his most famous work, *Faust*. It is strange that he would pick on Goethe's great epic poem and write one of the most popular operas in the world. Here was a deeply religious man who wrote church music most of his life composing a master-work about an old man who sells his soul to the devil in return for becoming young again!

The opera is filled with marvelous music for both the hero and heroine and great choruses of which the "Soldier's Chorus" is the most famous. (*Faust* became so popular that the Metropolitan chose it to open its doors for the first time on October 22, 1883.)

Yet religion and its mysteries continued to be Gounod's passion. He returned to Paris in 1875 (at fifty-seven) where he wrote more Masses and religious songs. (The best known is his great *Ave Maria*.)

Finally, he began writing a Requiem—a Mass for the dead. Could it have been a feeling of his own end that had come to mind? Was he (as with another renowned composer we will meet later on) writing his own Requiem? Who can tell?

But on October 15, 1893, while he was hard at work on this music, he suffered a stroke. He was unconscious for three days, and then, at the age of seventy-five, he passed away.

Today, although he wrote nine operas, only *Romeo et Juliette* and *Faust* remain to be enjoyed by opera lovers everywhere.

As we leave the ancient city of Verona, with its colorful medieval flags flying, its narrow streets filled with strollers, vendors, young lovers. . . . we pass the former House of Capulet. We peer into the courtyard. High above is still the famous balcony, the scene of bygone joys and sadness. And there, at the end of the small garden, is a life-size bronze statue of the little girl who grew up to be the most famous teenager the world has ever known.

So far we have visited the Vienna of 1874 and the Verona of the 1300's. Where else can the world of opera take us? Most anywhere, but right now our heart is set on Spain. Three hundred years have passed since the days of Romeo and Juliet. It is the seventeenth century and the spot is the peaceful city of Seville. We are taken there by the young composer Gioacchino Rossini (Jo-a-KEE-no Ro-SEE-nee) who, *in only thirteen days,* wrote the masterpiece opera...

3

Il Barbiere di Siviglia

(Eel Bahr-BYEH-ray dee See-VEEL-ya)

Gioacchino Rossini, born in February 1792, was in his early twenties, full of the spirit and comic outlook he placed in his music, when he wrote *The Barber of Seville*. His own life had a tragi-comical air about it and perhaps that helped him to speedily create this happy work.

His own father was known, in the little Italian village of Pesaro, as a "character." Here he was many things: town crier, slaughterhouse inspector, and sometime revolutionary—very much a jack-of-all-trades, similar to one of the main characters we will soon meet in the opera. He also played the horn. Gioacchino's mother was a soprano and so they toured local theatres where the young boy learned to play horn, viola, piano and studied voice. He was, therefore, the only major opera composer (besides Charles Gounod and Gaetano Donizetti) to have been a trained singer.

The Barber is yet another story about young lovers, but this time with much fun and mischief. Before the curtain rises we hear one of Rossini's most popular overtures. It has what a very important writer (Stendhal) described as a "peculiar verve, a certain stirring rapidity which lightens the spirit...." We hear the sweetness of the violins...the rousing crescendo of these same instruments and the power of the full orchestra. Soon there are five notes repeated. These become the "trademark" of this lively piece. Finally, with a growing volume of sound, the overture comes to a close with three grand chords.

ACT I

The curtain goes up on a square in Seville, showing Doctor Bartolo's house on the left. It is just before dawn and a group of musicians, led by Fiorello, servant of the Count Almaviva, are introduced to the Count who is wrapped up in a mantle. He has fallen in love with pretty Rosina, the ward of Don Bartolo, and is trying to sing her a serenade.

Fiorello, a music master, warns everybody to be very quiet and to follow him. The musicians comically repeat the warning and state that they are here. The Count calls to Fiorello who answers that he's right there, too.

"What about your friends?"

"They're all ready."

"Good! Be very quiet...."

The musicians tune their instruments. There is a fanfare and then with a guitar accompaniment the Count begins the serenade. He has a lyric tenor voice.

"Here in the smiling sky, the dawn is breaking...and you have not yet arisen...my sweet love...Oh...I see that dear vision...Oh, moment divine...which has no equal!"

Unfortunately, nothing happens—no Rosina, no light, no opening of doors.

"Hey, Fiorello!"

"My lord?"

"Tell me, have you seen her?"

"No, sir."

The Count is crushed. Fiorello reminds him that it's getting light. The musicians feel sorry for him. Well, since his serenade was a failure, the Count gives up and tells the others to leave. He gives Fiorello a purse so that he can pay off the musicians and sadly says, "Your instruments, your songs, I no longer need."

Now, of course, he wants them to leave as fast and as quietly as possible. But they're so grateful for having been given the job that they start a whole chorus of, "A thousand thanks...to a gentleman of great quality...." They go on and on in spite of the efforts of Fiorello and the Count to get rid of them—and above all, to keep them quiet!

At last they go. Fiorello also leaves. The Count is alone. But not for long! We hear a voice happily la-la-la-ing. The Count hides. In an instant, Figaro, the Barber of Seville, enters with his guitar and immediately introduces himself to anyone who will listen!

> "Make way for the city's jack-of-all-trades!...rushing to his shop, since dawn is already here! Ah, what a beautiful life! What wonderful pleasures for a barber of quality!"

Figaro, in one of the most well-known of all baritone *arias,* goes on to tell us how terrific he is, ready for anything, day or night. He is a master of his art. Then, of course, there are extra services he performs...not just cutting hair. For the ladies...la, la, la...(he sings lightly). For cavaliers...la, la, la...(he sings darkly).

> "Everybody calls me! Everybody wants me! Here a

shave...there a wig...take this note...what a crowd! Hey Figaro! I'm here! Hey Figaro! I'm here! Here a Figaro...there a Figaro...Figaro up...Figaro down... everybody wants me—wonderful Figaro! I sure am lucky to be...the jack-of-all-trades of the city!''

And so Figaro lets it be known that without him nothing of importance can really happen in Seville. The Count calls to him. Figaro immediately recognizes "Your Excellency!" The Count tells him to be quiet since no one knows him here, and he wants it that way. "Fine," says Figaro, "I'll leave." But the Count doesn't want that either. He is thinking of getting Figaro to help him. "What brings you here, so fat and sassy?" asks the Count.

"Poverty, sir!"

"Go on...you scoundrel!"

"Thank you," exclaims Figaro happily.

"Are you still being clever?"

"And how! How come you're in Seville?"

The Count explains that he saw a beautiful "flower" on the Prado. The daughter of a certain silly doctor. He fell in love with her at first sight, and so left home and country to hover around her balcony.

"*This* balcony? Well," Figaro continues, "you're very lucky. In fact, the cheese fell right on the macaroni!"

"What do you mean?"

"Well, here, I happen to be the barber, wig-maker, surgeon, botanist, druggist, veterinarian; in other words, I'm the major-domo of the whole place!"

The Count is delighted, and becomes even more so, when he is told that the girl is not the doctor's daughter but only his ward.

Suddenly the balcony window opens, and the two quickly hide. At the same time Doctor Bartolo comes out of the house. He gives his servant last minute instructions, telling him that he will return soon, not to let anyone inside, and that if Don Basilio comes around let him wait. As Bartolo locks the door he mutters that he is going to hurry up and marry the girl this very day!

The Count is bitter. But he wants to know who this Don Basilio is. Figaro tells him that he's a busy-body match-maker, a two-faced good-for-nothing, who never has any money. Lately he's become a music teacher to Rosina.

"And now," continues Figaro, "you've got to sing Rosina a pretty song in which you will explain your intentions."

When the Count starts to object, Figaro begins to lose patience. So the Count says that he'll try. He cautiously sings a sweet serenade in which he tells Rosina that his name is Lindoro, that he loves her, and that he wishes to marry her.

Rosina finally appears on the balcony and dreamily tells "her dear one" to continue his song. The Count, now in "seventh heaven," sings that he's sincere in his love, but that he can't give her riches, only a faithful love. Rosina starts to answer in the same way when she suddenly shrieks and leaves the balcony. The Count is flustered. But Figaro simply comments on the obvious: someone has entered her room and she's gone inside.

The Count is beside himself with love for Rosina. He must see her. He must speak to her. Will Figaro help him? Of course he will, but these days...Oh sure, he'll be well paid...lots of gold!

Naturally, this is all that Figaro wants to hear. He starts a lively tune. The thought of gold sets his mind to working, and all kinds of ideas begin to "erupt."

Finally, Figaro advises the Count that he must disguise himself as a soldier. A soldier? Yes, sir! A regiment is expected today...and he can insist on being lodged in the house! (In those days it was customary to ask house-holders to take in soldiers as boarders; it was called being billeted.)

Figaro is carried away with his own inventive genius. Soon he stops with another thought. The Count must pretend to be *drunk!*

"Drunk?" asks the Count. "But why...?"

Figaro explains, singing to music that imitates the swaying of a drunk.

"Because her guardian would be more likely to trust someone who doesn't know what he's doing!"

Both of them agree that this is a great idea. They also agree to meet later, and with a final duet, in which the Count dreams of meeting Rosina while Figaro dreams of the clinking gold, they part. Figaro goes into Bartolo's house, while the Count leaves to become a "soldier."

The scene changes. It's a room inside the house. Rosina is holding a letter. After a short musical introduction, she sings one of the opera's best-loved arias: "The voice I heard a short time ago..."

How thrilled she is to be head over heels in love with "Lindoro." She may be docile and respectful and obedient...*BUT*...if she is crossed by her guardian—prevented from loving Lindoro—she can be a real viper! And (she sings repeatedly) she has a hundred tricks to play before "they" get *their* way!

But how can she get a letter to him? Then she remembers that she saw Lindoro talking to Figaro! Perhaps he's the one to help their love. No sooner does she say this than Figaro enters the room. (Could he have been listening?)

"Oh, good day, young lady!"

"Good day, Signor Figaro!"

"And how are things?"

"I'm dying of boredom!"

"The devil you say! You...a beautiful girl full of spirit!"

"Ah, you make me laugh! What good is that if I'm shut up in four walls...as if in a grave...."

Figaro is about to have a talk with her about this when Rosina hears her guardian's footsteps. Figaro quickly hides.

"What a nice fellow," says Rosina.

In contrast to this Don Bartolo comes in calling Figaro all kinds of names! He exclaims, "They don't come any worse!"

"Have you seen him?" he then demands of Rosina.

"Why?"

"Because I *want to know*!" he shouts.

"All right," says Rosina. "Yes, I've seen him...I like him...I even think he's handsome!" Then (under her breath) she says, "Croak with rage, wicked old man!" And out she goes!

"Isn't she sweet?" mutters Don Bartolo.

Then he reflects that the more he loves her, the more she despises him. It must be that Figaro! He'll pay for this!

At this point, in comes Don Basilio. Now *he's* a sight to see! Tall and thin, with a long black frock, an enormous wide-brimmed hat, and a speckled red handkerchief drooping out of his back pocket.

Don Bartolo tells him he has come just in time. Basilio must arrange to get the marriage over with as soon as possible. Basilio says that that is exactly why he has arrived. You must keep a secret, he warns Bartolo.

"Count Almaviva is here!"

"You mean Rosina's lover?"

"Exactly!"

"The devil...something must be done!"

"Of course...but quietly..."

Don Basilio has a plan to get rid of the Count Almaviva. It is to start a rumor, a slander...to make everybody believe that he is no good. Within four days he'll be thrown out of town!

(This conversation now leads up to an aria by Don Basilio,

in his *bass* voice, in which he describes to Bartolo exactly what slander is and how it works!)

"La calunnia (slander or calumny)," he sings, "is like a gentle little breeze..."

... which glides from place to place, from person to person...entering the mind, growing bigger and bigger...until finally like the explosion of a cannon...it crashes around the poor slandered one...trampling him down and beating him to death!

As this whole thing is being dramatized by Don Basilio, his listener (Bartolo) is being scared out of his wits. But he soon recovers and comments that all that may be so, but meanwhile time is flying by.

"So let's go to my room and prepare the marriage contract at once!"

Of course, Figaro has heard everything and as soon as Rosina enters the room he tells her all about Don Bartolo's plot to marry her right away.

"Well," declares Rosina, "he's very wrong about that!"

She coyly asks Figaro about the young man she saw from the balcony.

"Oh," says Figaro, "he's a fine fellow, here to study and find his fortune!"

"Oh," says Rosina, "he'll make it...."

"I doubt that very much. You see, he has one great fault..."

"A great fault?..."

"He is dying of love...." (Now Rosina catches on and begins to play the game.)

"Tell me," she asks, "does this loved one live far away?"

"Oh no," says Figaro, giving her a long glance..."only two steps..."

"But is she pretty?"

Yes, this mystery girl is very pretty. In fact, he describes Rosina herself, who is quite sure where all this is leading. But she continues playing the little game and asks about this unknown girl's name.

He teases her by saying that she has a lovely name.

"Her name is Ro..."

"Ro..."

"and si..."

"si...," repeats Rosina.

"Ro-si...," prompts Figaro.

And then together they pronounce the name "Rosina!"

Rosina sings that she knew it was her all along. She does this with a flourish, with many graceful notes (called *fioritura*). And, of course, Figaro answers the same way as they continue a delightful duet about when she will meet her lover "Lindoro."

Figaro suggests that she write Lindoro a note asking him to meet her. She hesitates prettily, then much to Figaro's surprise takes out the note which she had already written! The duet ends with both reaching beautiful high notes; Rosina looking forward to meeting her love, while Figaro is wagging his head saying, "Women, women, how can you guess what they're thinking?" And on this note Figaro leaves.

Don Bartolo enters. He is very suspicious and asks Rosina why Figaro was lurking about. She fibs that Figaro was talking about French fashion and about his daughter Marcellina. "Oh, yeah?" thinks Bartolo.

"What about your ink-stained fingers?"

"Oh, I burned myself and I used the ink as medicine!"

"How about the writing paper...there are only five sheets instead of six!"

"Oh, I used one to wrap up some candy for Marcellina!"

Well, Don Bartolo doesn't believe a word of this. He sings

a little aria, accompanied lightly by violins, saying that Rosina had better make up more convincing stories if she is to fool *him!* He goes on to say that he will instruct the servants not to let her out of the house when he leaves. In fact, he will have her locked in her room altogether! And so they both go out glaring at each other.

In comes Berta, the house maid. She has her feather duster and is about to do some work when there is a knock on the door. We hear the Count's voice shouting to have the door opened.

"I'm coming...I'm coming! Who the devil can this be?"

She opens the door and in staggers the Count disguised as a soldier.

"Hey...anybody home? Hey!"

It doesn't take long for Bartolo to rush in. He spots the soldier.

"What an ugly face," he says. "And he's drunk, too!"

The "soldier" continues to shout, "Hey, isn't anybody home!" Finally Bartolo gets his attention and asks him what he wants.

"Oho...wait a minute...you're Doctor *Balordo....*"

"What Balordo?"

"Ah...Bertoldo!"

"What Bertoldo...Doctor *Bartolo,* Doctor *Bartolo!*"

"Ah, fine...Doctor Barbaro...fine...Doctor Barbaro!"

While this intentional mix-up is going on, with Bartolo getting madder and madder, the Count is looking around for Rosina.

She tip-toes in and the Count spots her. She wonders what this crazy soldier is doing here. At the first chance the soldier tells her that he's *Lindoro.* She's startled and quickly warns him to be careful. When Bartolo sees Rosina he tells her to leave the room at once!

"I'm going...don't shout!"

"I'm going, too," says the soldier.

"Where, where to?" asks Bartolo, trying not to lose his head.

"To my bedroom!"

Well, that's the last thing Bartolo wants him to do. After all he is *exempt* from taking in soldiers! He shows the drunk a paper that in fact does excuse him from boarding soldiers.

Meanwhile, the Count, feeling that he will really have to leave, asks Rosina to drop her handkerchief on top of a note which he will let fall to the floor.

However, Bartolo catches them and demands to see the letter! But the soldier gallantly hands the letter and the handkerchief to Rosina. Rosina sings her "thank you. . .thank you" which makes Bartolo explode.

"Thank you nothing! Give me that paper!"

"But it's only the laundry list. . ."

At this point Don Basilio, the old humbug music teacher, arrives with Berta.

Somehow Rosina actually has been able to switch the note for a laundry list! Bartolo is mortified. How could he have made such a mistake?

Basilio starts a singing exercise, "Sol-do-re-mi-fa-sol-mi-la-fa-sol-do—what kind of a mess do we have here?"

Now everybody starts to sing at once. Berta says that she's stunned with confusion. Rosina complains about how mistreated she is. The Count threatens Bartolo for hurting Rosina. They're all trying to keep him from giving Bartolo a good smack! And in the midst of all this Figaro comes in with a basin under his arm.

"Stop! What's going on here. . .there's so much noise. . .you've got the attention of half the city!"

This starts another round of accusations and bickering and name-calling.

"I'm going to kill him!" shouts the soldier.

All this stops quickly when there's a knock on the door. It's the police! Actually it's an Officer of the Guard with his men.

"Stay where you are!"

"Don't anybody move!" sings the whole chorus.

They all have a comical combination of excuses—ending with the officer placing the "soldier" under arrest!

"What!!!" shouts the Count.

He swiftly takes the officer aside and shows him the order of a Grandee of Spain. Without a word the officer signals to his men to leave. Everybody else stands there shocked!

Here, there is a marvelous quartet, to a somewhat mechanical rhythm, in which they all repeat the same words: "Cold and motionless...like a statue...I have no breath to breathe...!"

Confusion builds on more confusion. Finally, the members of the full chorus state that their poor brains are so filled with stunning confusion that they are all bordering on insanity!

The violins play, the *celeste* rings out its sweet notes, and the full orchestra joins in to end this uproarious first act.

ACT II

Here we are in Doctor Bartolo's living room. There's a grand piano covered with sheet music. We find the Doctor feeling sorry for himself.

"Look at my fate—that soldier is not even known by the entire regiment. I'll bet the Count Almaviva sent him here to check whether Rosina loves him. One can't even be safe in one's own house!"

Suddenly there's another knock on the door.

"Come in; I'm home!"

And in comes the Count now disguised as a music master! He

looks a little like a young minister, and starts piously singing, "Peace and happiness be with you...." Bartolo thanks him graciously and asks him to make himself at home. The Count continues his monotonous, "Happiness and peace for a thousand years..." The doctor politely accepts these good wishes, but begins to think that the face is familiar! Of course, the Count assures himself that this new disguise will surely fool the old fellow.

"Peace and happiness..."

"I heard you!" shouts Doctor Bartolo. ("My Heavens, what a bore!")

But the Count continues with his repeated good wishes, resulting in a very funny duet ending with Bartolo complaining of having the worst luck in the world. Finally, he gets the Count to shut up and asks him to identify himself.

"Why, I'm Don Alonzo—professor of music and Don Basilio's pupil!"

"So what?"

Well, "Don Alonzo" goes on to explain that his boss, Don Basilio, is sick and therefore has sent him to give Rosina her piano lesson. Raising his voice in the hopes of alerting Rosina somewhere in the house, he tells Bartolo that he actually comes from Count Almaviva. The poor Doctor nods but asks him to speak more softly. Then the Count gets an idea! He knows how to get on the Doctor's good side. He reveals that a certain note fell into his hands proving that Rosina has written to Almaviva! If he could get together with the girl he could make her believe that Almaviva is really unfaithful to her—claiming that the note to the Count really comes from his mistress!

"Aha!" exclaims Bartolo, "you really prove that you're Basilio's pupil. I get it! It will be a slander, a calumny!"

So Bartolo goes to get Rosina. The minute she spots the "music master" she's so surprised that she gives a muffled scream. Of course, the Don wants to know what happened; she quickly tells him that she had a cramp in her foot.

Rosina joins her lover with great pleasure. What would she like to sing? Oh the song from the "The Useless Precaution." So the piano accompaniment begins and Rosina (through the made-up song) tells of how much in love she is, but that a ruthless tyrant always keeps her guarded.

"Oh, Lindoro, come and save me for pity's sake!"

"Lindoro" at the piano gets the message. Rosina is not to worry because he will rescue her soon.

"What a beautiful voice!"

"A thousand thanks!"

Bartolo agrees, but he's not too happy with the words to *that* song and so proceeds to sing another one that tells of his love for Rosina.

Meanwhile, Figaro has entered and is imitating him behind his back. Bartolo soon discovers him and angrily wants to know what he is doing here.

"What am I here for—to give you a shave!"

"I don't want a shave—come back tomorrow!"

"I can't; I'm too busy with the Marquise Andronica... Count Bombe...and so on."

So they argue back and forth until Bartolo finally gives in. He takes out a bunch of keys. He's going to get the towels and will be right back. This is just what Figaro has been waiting for. He asks Rosina which one of the keys in the bunch opens the balcony windows. The newest one! It isn't long before Bartolo hurries back muttering that he was foolish to leave Figaro behind since he doesn't trust him anyway. So he gives *Figaro* the keys and tells *him* to get the supplies he needs. While the doctor is starting to get very suspicious about everything that's been happening, we hear a tremendous crash. This does the trick—and Don Bartolo rushes out again! Lindoro now has a chance to ask Rosina to trust him completely. Of course she does!

When Bartolo returns, followed by Figaro, the Count asks him, "Well?"

"He's broken everything...six plates, eight glasses, a tureen...."

Figaro secretly shows the Count that he has "borrowed" the key to the window. But as Bartolo is being prepared for shaving, both Rosina and the Count spy Don Basilio (of all people) arriving.

So the Count's plot now has a big bug in it. How to get rid of Don Basilio? The Count gets Bartolo's ear and warns him that since Basilio doesn't know about the phony letter, he might spill the beans.

"You're right!"

"With such a fever, Don Basilio, who told you you could go out?" asks the Count.

"What fever?"

"What do you mean?...You're as yellow as a corpse!"

"Yellow as a corpse?"

(Now Figaro gets into the act.)

"What a trembling you have! You must have scarlet fever!"

(The Count secretly gives Basilio a bag of money.)

"Go buy some medicine...you don't want to get worse!...."

By this time Basilio is beginning to think that they have all gone crazy. So when all four, together, tell him to quickly get to bed, Basilio shouts that he's not deaf...and stop begging him.

Now the Count tells him he has turned green. With this, Basilio (especially since he has just been bribed) decides to go. The following little scene is one of the funniest in the opera.

Basilio, taking his own sweet time, bids them all good night. Each in turn wishes *him* good night. He repeats and repeats his "good nights" until they can't stand it! Finally, asking them not to shout for pity's sake, Basilio gradually leaves. Everyone breathes a big sigh of relief.

With Basilio finally gone, Figaro starts on Don Bartolo. He tries to help Rosina and the Count by covering Don Bartolo with hot shaving towels. But, although Almaviva succeeds in telling Rosina that he and Figaro will pick her up from the balcony at midnight, he doesn't get to explain that in order to carry off his disguise, he was forced to make up a story about her letter. At the word "disguise," Bartolo suddenly realizes that they are plotting against him!

"Out you scoundrels or I'll kill you!"

But all three—Rosina, the Count and Figaro—get together to calm him down, telling him that he's delirious, and that he should stop shouting! It's no use...Bartolo continues to rage at them and finally chases them all out.

The room is now empty. In strolls the maid, Berta. She has her trusty feather duster and as she begins to dust, in time with the music, she sings a comical little aria that often stops the show.

"What a suspicious old man...there's always arguing... shouting and noise in this house...."

She goes on to comment about the typical lover's triangle: the old man, the beautiful young maiden, and the handsome young man.

"But what is this thing called love...which makes everyone delirious...poor me, even *I* feel it...an old maid...I shall die in desperation!"

And out she goes.

By now it is night. As luck would have it, there's a big rainstorm blowing. Violins play quietly, but soon the full orchestra begins to thunder with storm music. Flashes of lightning appear. Soon the balcony window is opened. Figaro, carrying a lantern and wrapped in a cloak, climbs in followed by the Count. Where is Rosina? There she is! But it is an angry Rosina that the Count discovers.

"You pretended love. . .in order to turn me over to the will of that vile Count Almaviva. . .!"

This news comes as a big relief to the Count. He at last introduces himself. . ., "I am Almaviva, I am not Lindoro!"

With this secret finally out, Rosina is pleasantly surprised to say the least! There is a fanfare as she wakes up to her good fortune.

"With surprise and contentment I am almost delirious!"

While the lovers are ecstatic about it all, Figaro is congratulating himself on how talented he is. . .what a great stroke of genius he has brought about!

To the sound of violins the Count proposes to Rosina. She is no longer just his lady love but she can look forward to becoming his adored bride!

They go into a most happy duet while Figaro, hovering about, is trying to get them to "Hurry up!. . .this is no time for sighs. . . ."

But it is too late. Figaro sees two people and a lantern at the door outside. There is a great deal of excitement, musically and vocally. They really don't know *what* to do. Then in a hushed, spritely little tune they decide that they will be very quiet and go back down the ladder at the balcony.

"Quiet, quiet, softly, softly. . .Let's not have any confusion. . . . With the ladder at the balcony we shall quickly get away!"

But suddenly Figaro finds the ladder gone! Now what? Before they can think of anything, in strides Don Basilio with his notary. This instantly gives Figaro a bright idea. Without a twitch, he greets the notary and tells him to settle the contract between the Count Almaviva and. . .*"my niece. . . ."*

When Basilio asks about Don Bartolo the Count quickly takes him aside, gives him the ring from his finger and warns him to be quiet. As Basilio begins to protest, the Count assures him that if he doesn't accept the ring... "he will be exchanging it for two bullets in the head!"

"My goodness! I'll take the ring. Who signs?"

"Here we are. The witnesses are Figaro and Don Basilio. And this is my bride."

"Hurray!" sings Figaro.

In comes Don Bartolo!

"Stop everybody! Arrest them...arrest them!"

"Your name, sir?" asks the officer.

"I am the Count Almaviva...."

Well this is the last straw! Bartolo finally gives up!

"In other words...I'm always wrong...." He turns to Don Basilio, "You too, betrayed me...."

"Ah..." notes Basilio, "that Count...has arguments for which there are no answers."

"Then, to be *sure* they got married...," continues Don Bartolo, "I took away the ladder from the balcony!"

However, he finally accepts the whole affair, and with the orchestra coming to full life, they all sing to the happiness of the newlyweds...ending up with the repeated wish, "May love and faith be eternally yours!"

The voices and orchestra swell to a hearty climax...seven fast chords followed by two full longer ones echo throughout the house.

THE CURTAIN FALLS

And so this witty, melodious *opera buffa* (comic work) comes to an end once again. Written when Rossini was in his early twenties, and first performed in Rome's Argentina Theater on February 20, 1816, *The Barber* has been on one stage after another ever since delighting untold millions with its humorous situation and, of course, its immortal music. Rossini took his libretto from three satires by the French playright, PierreAugustin Caron de Beaumarchais; then sat down with his librettist, Cesare Sterbini, and created a masterpiece.

The great Ludwig van Beethoven himself was so taken with the opera that he urged Rossini to compose "more Barbers."

Yet Rossini had his serious side as well. In fact, one of his best serious works is the truly grand opera *William Tell,* written when he was only thirty-seven. By this time he had moved to Paris where he was to live the remainder of his life. Strangely, he never wrote another opera, though he lived the life of a Parisian *bon vivant* (enjoying good food and drink) until the age of seventy-six.

We've already done a good bit of traveling with our operas, going from one country to another, as well as leaping across the centuries. However, our next trip is also in Spain; in fact, inside the same city. But the Seville we are about to visit in nothing like the Seville of *The Barber.*

It is in another section of town, not nearly as nice as the one we have seen. Imagine, the most important thing there is a cigarette factory! But let's not judge too fast. We're being "taken" there by a man named Georges Bizet (Beezay), and that makes a lot of difference. This famous composer takes us into the strange world of Carmen—the fatalistic, moody, sensual, suicidal, and unfaithful gypsy girl whose own wild spirit brings her to a tragic end. And we live the story through the music of the young Georges Bizet, creator of the greatest French lyric opera of the nineteenth century.

At the age of ten this gifted writer, born and raised in Paris, entered the Conservatory. By age seventeen he had written the Symphony in C Major. At nineteen he won the highest award of the Conservatory, the Prix de Rome (the Roman Prize).

He loved Rome. "My senses are enthralled by Italian music— facile, idle, amorous, lascivious and passionate all at once!"

Without realizing it he had described the music that he himself was to write.

The opera story we are about to enjoy was taken from a popular short novel by Prosper Merimee, written in 1845. He was a journalist and had heard this true story directly from Don Jose Lizzarrabengoa, as he awaited his fate in his death cell. The libretto was written by Ludovic Halevy and Henri Meilhac and the finished work was first performed at the Opera Comique on March 3, 1875. And now let's see why the audience on that evening in Paris was so shocked by the mocking gypsy girl called . . .

4

Carmen

Before the curtain goes up the orchestra starts with lively music that leads into the "Toreador Song" heard later in the second act. There's the repeated crashing of cymbals. Then slowly the violins bring in the "passion" theme linking Carmen and Corporal Don Jose. It builds and builds until a final, sudden chord tells us of the fateful end of the story.

ACT I

When the curtain rises we see a square with a cigarette factory and a guardhouse. Soldiers are taking it easy here and there. Morales (More-AHL-ess), the Corporal of the Guard, is just as lazy as they are. They all sing about the people passing back and forth, and how funny-looking they are. Shortly, Morales spots a young girl who seems to be looking for someone. The other soldiers perk up too. The girl looks lost.

"What are you looking for, my beauty?" asks Morales.

"I'm looking for a corporal."

"Well, here I am!"

"My corporal is named Don Jose...do you know him?"

Well, of course, they all know Don Jose, but he won't be there till the changing of the guard—so, in the meantime...

But the girl, Micaela (Mee-ka-AY-la), struggles free of the surrounding soldiers and runs off. "The bird has flown...."

So the soldiers go back to their pastime again, making fun of the people strolling by. Off-stage we hear a bugle blaring. In a few moments the new guard arrives with Corporal Don Jose (Dohn Josay) and Lieutenant Zuniga (ZOO-nee-gah). They're being followed by a group of boys who make believe that they, too, are changing the guard. They sing to marching music and tramp around, copying the movement of the soldiers.

Meanwhile, Morales tells Jose that a pretty girl was just there looking for him. From the description—blue skirt and braided hair—Don Jose knows it is Micaela. As the old guard leaves, the young boys follow them out still singing their song...gradually fading away.

Zuniga walks over to Don Jose, who is fixing his gear. He wants to know about the girls in the factory.

"Is that where they work?"

"Yes, sir, and you sure won't find a worse bunch of girls anywhere."

"But are they at least good-looking?"

"I don't know, sir. I'm not really interested...."

Zuniga remarks that *he* knows who Jose is interested in—it's that pretty girl in the blue skirt...what about that?

"I say it's true...I love her...and as for the factory

girls...here they are...judge for yourself.''

The factory bell rings. The men hanging around sing that they are there to take up with the girls if they can.

"Just look at them...bold flirts...cigarettes hanging from their lips...!"

In a lazy chorus the girls talk about the pleasure of cigarette smoke...and how it lazily rises into the air. The drifting smoke is like the "sweet talk of lovers" which is nothing more than smoke that disappears!

The orchestra sounds a chord. The men ask where little Carmen is...and then they see her!

"Carmen...tell us when you will love us...!"

This is all that Carmen needs to start her famous "Habanera" (Ha-bahn-YER-a). With swaying hips (and a fast look at Don Jose, who isn't paying any attention to her) she asks:

"When will I love you...? I don't really know...Love is a wild bird...that no one can tame...."

She prefers a fellow who pays no attention (looking at Don Jose). We soon see that this is the worst of the "loose" girls that Don Jose spoke about.

"Love is a gypsy...not governed by any law...If you don't love me...I love you...but if I love you—*watch out!*"

Throughout Carmen's song, both the girls and the men repeat her wild ideas: love is fickle, love goes, comes back, and leaves again. Near the end of her swinging, sensuous aria, Carmen (annoyed by Don Jose's not caring) throws the flower she has pinned to her dress at his feet...and runs away.

The orchestra emphasizes this...and shortly, to the sound of two bass notes, the scene ends.

Jose is now alone. He picks up the flower. He starts to think. (Carmen's tricks are working.)

"This flower...made me feel as if I was hit by a bullet!

It's pretty...and that girl...if there are such things as witches...she surely is one of them!''

At this point, Micaela comes back. (Bizet was certainly thinking of the big difference between these two women.) If Carmen is a witch, Micaela, then is an angel.

Jose is glad to see her. Micaela softly tells him that his mother has sent her...to give him a letter and a little money. And something else. She shyly says that she is also to give him a kiss...from his mother.

"A kiss for her son...Jose, I will give it to you as I promised."

A haunting theme, that will be repeated, now starts a duet in which they sing of "... dear memories of home...his mother...and the land where he was born...." To Jose his mother's letter and kiss came just in time to ward off "the devil...the danger...and save her son!"

Micaela is puzzled by these words. But Jose brushes them away and talks of her return home. He wants his mother to be proud of him.

"... Tell her that...and give her this kiss from me...."

He kisses her gently. Micaela promises and then they once again sing together of their memories of home...mother...and their native countryside.

Jose is now about to read his mother's letter. Micaela suspects that she is in the letter so she tells Jose that she is leaving but will return.

Micaela was right. We hear Jose promising to do as his mother tells him.

"I love Micaela, I will make her my wife."

An uproar stops his thinking (which also includes ideas about that gypsy witch). The cigarette girls rush out of the factory, yelling and screaming. Zuniga comes out of the guardhouse to see what's happening.

One bunch of girls is screaming that it was little Carmen's (Carmencita's) fault. Another blames the girl Manuelita. Carmencita insulted Manuelita! No she didn't! Yes she did! They both grabbed each other's hair!

Zuniga, fed up with this whole mess, orders Jose to take two men and go inside to find out what really happened and who's to blame. At this, the yelling starts all over again.

"It was Carmencita who hit first! No, it was Manuelita...."

As Jose comes out dragging Carmen along, we hear the musical theme that will be connected with these two. Jose reports that a woman has been wounded.

"By whom?"

"By her, of course."

Zuniga turns to Carmen. "Well—what have you got to say?"

Carmen, swings her hips and starts to hum a tune. In a throaty voice she sings, "Hit me, burn me,...I'll tell you nothing...." Slowly, sensuously she defies everything—"fire, the sword, heaven itself!"

Zuniga has had about enough of this. He orders Jose to tie her up and drag her off to jail. As he leaves to write out the order he notes that it's too bad. That Carmen is really something...but "she's got to be taught a lesson."

When Carmen finds herself alone with Jose, she goes to work. He's not going to obey Zuniga because he (Jose) will do whatever she wants him to..."because you love me...!" (Yes, that flower that she tossed him, has already begun to work!)

"Don't talk to me anymore...I forbid it!"

Here the woodwinds and violins turn on their charm just as Carmen does. She invites Jose to meet her at her friend's place. There at Lillas Pastia's she'll dance the *seguidilla* (folk dance) and drink *manzanilla* (sherry). But she gets bored being alone. So she'll take a lover along. Here it is the weekend...who wants to have a good time...who wants to love her?

As Carmen continues to tempt Jose, he begins to weaken. Finally, he gives in. Carmen gives him a plan. When Zuniga comes out with the order, Jose will start to take her away. But in a moment, she'll give him a hefty push and make him fall. . . "and leave the rest to me!"

As they walk away, she seductively sings again some lines of the "Habanera." Suddenly she pushes Jose to the ground, breaks free and runs off laughing. The girls join in. . . the orchestra builds, cymbals clash—and five full chords end the colorful scene as the curtain falls.

ACT II

Before it rises again, there's a light, lively little tune by the orchestra. It's the soldier's song, soon to be sung by Don Jose. The scene is Lillas Pastia's tavern. It's a hangout for soldiers, gypsy girls and, more importantly, the meeting place for a gang of smugglers. There's dancing, flirting and drinking. Carmen slowly starts to sing about gypsy dancing. She talks of the drums beating, the guitars strumming faster and faster. Her girl friends Frasquita and Mercedes join in with a tra-la-la. There's the tapping of heels of the Spanish Flamenco. The whole scene gets wilder and wilder, with Carmen leading the rest. Finally, in a whirling burst of tapping and singing, the dance ends.

Frasquita announces that Pastia has to close the tavern on orders from the magistrate. Zuniga, the officer, agrees to go. But he tries to get the girls to go with him. They refuse (having other things on their minds, such as meeting with Remendado and Dancairo, the bandit leaders).

Zuniga wants Carmen especially to go with him, telling her that if she still has a grudge against him for putting Jose in jail, well, she should know that he's free again. Carmen likes the idea that Jose is available, but before she can get rid of the others we hear the sound of cheering getting louder and louder.

"Hurrah for the toreador! Long live Escamillo (Ess-kah-MEE—yo)!"

Zuniga opens the door on the torchlight crowd. The cheers are for the winner of the Granada bullfight! In comes the hero of the day. Zuniga offers a toast. The crowd continues their cheering. Trumpets sound. The orchestra swings into one of the most familiar arias ever written, the *Toreador Song!*

Escamillo gives a toast saying "to toreadors and soldiers, both get pleasure from fighting!" Then he starts to tell them in his swashbuckling way about the bullring and fighting the bull!

"Be careful toreador, be careful. . . and remember dark eyes are watching you—love is waiting—so be on your guard!"

As Escamillo sings his exciting aria, the crowd sings with him, including Carmen and her friends.

"All of a sudden everyone is silent," sings Escamillo.

The bull charges. He strikes. A horse falls and rolls, trapping a picador! Soon the bull is bleeding from the *banderillos* (darts) stuck into him by the picadors. He's weakening! The time has come for the master stroke of the toreador! And with a stirring climax the song ends.

The dashing toreador turns to Carmen at once. He asks her name. Not wasting any time, Escamillo asks:

"What if I should tell you that I love you?"

"I'd say that you had better not!"

"That's not a very nice reply—but I have hopes. . . ."

". . .Hope is sweet. . .," replies Carmen, not caring one way or another.

Zuniga breaks in. Since she won't come with him, he will come back later. With that Escamillo and Zuniga leave. We hear the music of the *Toreador Song* again—then it fades away.

Meanwhile, the gang of smugglers gets down to business. They put their heads together to plan their next job. Dancairo thinks that things look good but they'll need the girls to go along.

In a brilliant mixture of all five voices, the leaders insist they need the girls, and the girls ask why.

"... When it comes to swindling, cheating and stealing ... it's always a good idea to have women along...."

So they finally agree—except for Carmen. To everybody's surprise, Carmen refuses. No amount of pleading will change her mind. Well, then, for heaven's sake, why not?

"...Because, at the moment, I'm in love...."

"What did she say?"

"She says she's in love!"

"Look here, Carmen, be serious...."

Well, this is an unexpected snag, but no amount of argument will change Carmen's mind.

"Who are you waiting for?"

"Oh just a poor soldier—who did me a favor..."

Off in the distance Jose is heard singing a soldier's song. He gets closer. Carmen's girl friends take a peek at him and think he's quite handsome.

The bandits—still trying to get Carmen to come along—suggest that she ask Jose to join the gang. She agrees to try.

"At last—it's you."

"Carmen!"

When the others leave the room, Carmen decides to dance for her "lover." She'll sing her own music. She begins—castanets clicking. (These are hollowed out wooden discs that are attached to the fingers and snapped together.)

But then there's a bugle call. It's the signal for all soldiers to get back to their beds. Carmen thinks that this makes perfect music for her dance. But Jose insists that he must go back to his barracks. Carmen is amazed and furious.

"To the barracks! For roll call!"

Well, this sets her off—she loses her temper—and Jose will regret it! She continues to mock him. She was stupid to be interested in *him!* She calls him a coward and a mere boy. Jose is deeply hurt—especially since he's hopelessly in love. But Carmen still scorns him.

"So you don't believe I love you?" Jose declares.

"Of course not!"

"Well, listen then..."

"No, no, no, no!"

Slowly the love theme that we've heard before begins. It introduces one of the most moving and melodious arias in opera.

"That flower that you threw at me," Jose recalls, "was with me in prison. And although it had faded it still kept its sweet odor."

She was always on his mind...until he couldn't stand it any more. He wanted only to see her again...to have her look at him once more.

"Carmen, I love you!"

The song ends. But Carmen is unmoved. If Jose really did love her he would follow her into the mountains. In a low, sexy voice she begins a refrain that is repeated again and again.

"There...in the mountains...there...you would follow me...if you loved me...."

Soon she winds her arms around his neck, always insisting, always tempting.

"You'd take me on your horse, and carry me away...!"

Jose is weakening; he tells her in a soft voice to be quiet. He is shocked to think that he would desert his flag...and his regiment! They are in the middle of angry "good-byes," when there's a knock on the door. It's Zuniga! The two men are after the same girl. Jose tells his superior officer to get out! They shout, calling names. Jose draws his sword! Carmen gets between them, calling for help.

Instantly, the gypsy band appears; the leaders quickly disarm

Zuniga. Trumpets blare. Then with sarcastic politeness the bandit leaders suggest that Zuniga "go for a little walk." Of course, Zuniga, faced with pistols has no choice.

"But watch out later on!"

"Are you one of us now?" asks Carmen, as she turns to Jose.

A spirited chorus now begins in which Carmen, along with her friends, sings of how wonderful a bandit's life can be. We hear again Carmen's tempting music. And as the chorus becomes louder, the orchestra full and strong, the voices reach a high note praising the open sky, the roving life—and above all, freedom!

And so, with Jose trapped into joining the bandits, his officer captive, his senses full of love for Carmen...the act ends.

Before the curtain rises on the third act we hear a sad, lyrical melody. The flute is heard alone, then the clarinet comes in and soon there are the violins. The tune rises and falls ending softly. This *entr'acte* (between the acts) piece sets the mood for the opening scene of...

ACT III

...which takes us to the smuggler's camp. We see a few of them asleep in their cloaks. Soon a familiar theme begins as more of the gypsy gang straggle in. The music takes on a kind of marching beat, repeated again and again. They sing of how there is a fortune "down there," but to be careful not to make a mistake! The chorus continues as Carmen and her friends arrive. Different voices say that theirs is a good business but you've got to be very careful of the danger on all sides.

Dancairo announces that they will rest here for about an hour while scouts make sure that the smuggled goods will get through. So the gang breaks up, some to sleep a bit longer. Jose is looking off in the distance in deep thought. Carmen wonders why.

"What are you looking at?"

"I was telling myself that down there is a nice old lady who thinks I'm an honest man. Well, she sure is wrong!"

Carmen demands to know who this woman is. Jose doesn't like her tone of voice, but tells her that it's his mother.

"Well, then, go back to her since this kind of life is not for you!"

"What? And leave you?"

"Sure!"

This angers Jose and he gives her a look "that could kill." He warns her not to talk about "separation" again. We hear the warning, fateful music.

"I suppose you would kill me," says Carmen. "What do I care...fate governs everything anyway."

This is the gypsy in Carmen and is one of the things that leads to her downfall. She goes right ahead, with her mind made up, even if it means she could die—because it is "fate...it is in the cards...!"

Sure enough, we see Frasquita and Mercedes happily singing about their future as they shuffle and turn over a deck of cards. They are asking the cards to tell them their fortune. "Speak...speak...!"

Frasquita sees a young lover who is mad about her. Mercedes sees a rich old man who talks of marriage. Frasquita's hero takes her up on his horse and carries her off...so that they will love forever. Mercedes dreams of gold and diamonds and other precious stones...and best of all, the old man dies and leaves her a rich widow!

So Frasquita speaks of a handsome leader of men who loves her while Mercedes can only think of wealth. Throughout all this the voices are singing to a spritely tune which is repeated as they think of the "fortune" that the cards are showing them.

Carmen interrupts them. She wants to try her luck. She turns the cards. Up comes the ace of spades! The card of death! That figures, she thinks, first me, then him—death for us both! Nothing can change fate. The orchestra thunders as the card of death appears again and again.

"Shuffle twenty times—the cards will still say death!"

With some very final notes from the orchestra, the scene comes to a close.

Dancairo reports that they will now try to get through the pass. He tells Jose to go up on a high rock as a lookout. He warns everybody that he spotted three customs men who will have to be removed. This doesn't bother the girls! All three sing a carefree song telling him that they will take care of the customs men. In fact, there might even be some arms around the waist and some flirting smiles. So leave those men to them! The music takes on a marching beat once again as the girls lead the way. As they get farther and farther away it fades and finally ends.

Now the woodwind instruments begin. The music introduces the good Micaela. She is looking for Jose. We hear the sad melody that becomes one of the most memorable of arias, Micaela's song. She is frightened to be there but she must find Jose. She will also see, close up, the one who lured Jose away from her and made him a criminal! She calls on the good Lord to protect her—as her voice soars—yes, protect her and keep her safe. The music ends softly.

She calls to Jose. But he is looking at something else. He raises his gun, takes aim and fires! Micaela, not knowing who he is shooting at, runs and hides. Shortly, a man appears. He complains to Jose that if he had aimed just a little lower he would have been killed. Jose demands to know who he is. Escamillo! Jose has heard of him and makes him welcome . . . "but you might have lost your life." Escamillo would gladly risk his life to see the girl he loves. Her name is Carmen! (You can imagine how this affects Jose!) Yes, she had a soldier lover but that's all gone now. After all, Carmen never has a lover more than six months!

Jose, with deadly calm, asks, "Do you understand that to carry off one of our gypsy girls you will have to pay...and the payment is given in knife stabbings!?'' Escamillo realizes he has actually been talking to the ''soldier'' that he had just mentioned! And as Jose is getting madder by the second, Escamillo can't help laughing at the whole thing.

''Here I come looking for a mistress...and I find her lover!''

He's still laughing when Jose, knife in hand, tells him to get ready to die. They start to fight. At first the bullfighter has the upperhand. But then...Jose snaps the blade of Escamillo's knife! As he is about to strike, Carmen rushes in and holds back his arm. Without missing a beat, Escamillo tells her he is overcome to think that he owes her his life. Then turning to Jose he remarks that they are finished for now, but that he's ready anytime to continue the fight.

Before the swashbuckling toreador goes he invites them all to the bullfight in Seville. He will put on a brilliant fight...and he expects (looking at Carmen) those who love him to be there!

And so, while the bandit leaders hold Jose back, Escamillo leaves to the faint tune of the *Toreador Song*.

Jose turns to Carmen and warns her to be careful. Don't get him (Jose) to the breaking point. Dancairo wants to start everybody going. Remendado suddenly discovers Micaela hiding among the rocks! That's a very nice surprise to find a pretty woman in their camp.

Jose is stunned and saddened to see Micaela, the girl he once was going to marry. Again we hear her theme, sweet and pleading. His mother wants him to come home.

''Go away, go away,'' Carmen tells Jose, ''this life is not for you!''

This angers him. To think that the woman he loves no longer wants him around. Soon the fate, or death, theme is heard.

''You're telling me to follow her so that you can run after your new lover! No, Carmen, I won't go...even if it costs me my life.''

Finally, desperately, Micaela tells him that his mother is actually dying. This then, changes his mind...and with a last harsh word to Carmen, he swears that they will meet again. The death music is again heard. Then, just as Micaela and Jose are about to leave, the voice of the toreador singing his rollicking song is heard in the distance! Carmen makes a move to go to him but Jose roughly blocks her way. And as we hear the song again, we know that fate has set the stage for the final tragedy. The act ends.

Before the next act begins the orchestra plays another between-the-acts musical piece. It opens with spirited chords. Then a woodwind instrument (the oboe) plays a lyrical tune...while the Spanish rhythm prepares us for the colorful scene ahead. The notes soften and disappear. The curtain is about to rise on the violent action of...

ACT IV

It is the square in Seville just outside the walls of the famous bullring. Street vendors are calling out their wares: fans to cool the spectators, wine, water...programs...cigarettes! We spot Lt. Zuniga with the girls Frasquita and Mercedes. He buys them some oranges. This busy crowd is typical of the color and gaiety of a Sunday afternoon in Seville.

Now the crowd shouts greetings to the "quadrilla of the Toreadors," soldier-like men with shining lances! We hear trumpets and cymbals in the orchestra and the now well-known marching music of the opera. The bullfight "parade" continues. There are the banderilleros! Look, look! The handsome picadors! Finally, Escamillo enters. Carmen is with him. While the crowd shouts their greeting to the brave and handsome toreador, we hear him tell Carmen—in a soft voice, "If you love me Carmen...you'll soon be proud of me...!"

"Ah...I love you Escamillo...more than anyone I have ever loved!"

At this point the mayor arrives and the crowd follows him into the bullring.

But before Carmen can leave, Frasquita comes to her and warns her that Jose has been seen. Carmen is not afraid—in fact she'll go and talk to him. "Take care...," warns her friend once again.

Sure enough Carmen goes to Jose.

"I was warned to fear for my life!"

Sorrowfully, Jose explains that he is not there to threaten her...but to plead with her to come back to him. He has sacrificed everything for her. Of course, Carmen will have none of that. In the duet that follows, Jose tells her how much he loves her...but Carmen does not love him any more—and what's worse, she now loves Escamillo. The orchestra falls silent.

"You no longer love me...?"

"No...."

"But we did love each other not long ago...don't leave me Carmen!"

"Carmen will never give in...I was born free...and I will die free!"

From the bullring the crowd is cheering. The bullfight is over! Carmen tries to get away. Jose is crushed.

"You want to join him...tell me, do you love him?"

"I love him! I love him...and even if I'm facing death I'll keep repeating I love him!"

Again we hear the familiar music of the opera as the crowd cheers the toreador.

"For the last time...will you come with me?"

"No...!" she shouts, as she takes his ring from her finger and throws it at his feet!

This is the final insult. Jose loses his head and with a desperate stroke he stabs Carmen to death! And while we are watching this tragedy the crowd in the arena is heard singing Escamillo's song. The violins play mournfully.

Others begin to gather around Don Jose.

"Arrest me...it is I who killed her...!"

As the music swells, Jose falls to his knees beside the girl he loved so much.

"Oh, Carmen...my beloved Carmen...!" he cries out.

And with the orchestra sounding two powerful chords, the tragic story of the wild and faithless gypsy girl comes to a dramatic close.

THE CURTAIN FALLS

Today, it is hard to believe that the people who first heard Bizet's music felt that it lacked melody. If there is one opera that "everybody" has heard (at least in part) it is *Carmen*. And it is, of course, the melodies that we remember!

That first night was a tragic disappointment for young Bizet. He had tried—and had succeeded—in creating a work of beauty that was true to life. But the public of that time was just not ready for a girl like Carmen.

Yet, curiosity got the best of them. The fact that this was a story about a rather loose woman didn't do the box-office any harm. In the next three months the opera was played thirty-seven times—an average of three times a week.

But in George Bizet's mind it was a failure. All his work, all the time spent in rehearsal...and for what? And so, on the third of June, 1875 even as the curtain was once again coming down on his masterpiece, Bizet died. His doctors said it was a blood clot. His friends claimed it was a broken heart. He was only thirty-seven years old!

He did not live to see how his *Carmen* finally triumphed in Paris. Although it played in Vienna, London and other cities, it was not until eight years after that disappointing first night, that the opera was performed at the Opera Comique once more...never again to leave the stages of all the great opera houses of the world.

And *we* don't seem to be able to leave Spain! Although we do some more leaping in time (for we will soon go back to the Spain—and Italy—of the 1700's) we stay once again in the romantic city of Seville.

The reason for this is to follow up on the theme expressed again and again in *Carmen*: the idea of the force of fate. If it's in the cards, it's bound to happen. Of course, not everyone believes this to be true. Some people firmly believe that you make your own "fate," while others think that forces beyond our control spin out the events in our lives. Well, whichever side you're on, you'll still be moved by the happenings and the music of an opera actually named *The Force of Destiny* (or in Italian, *La Forza del Destino*).

But before we hear the overture with its driving, repeated notes that seem to picture this force, let's meet a little boy who grew up to be one of the biggest giants in the world of music— Giuseppe Verdi. The name belongs to a youngster who, by the age of ten, had already shown signs of genius. Fortunately for him, and especially for us, he was surrounded by people who not only saw his genius but could do something about it. There was the shoe-maker, Pugnatta, who took young Verdi under his roof and with whom he lived in Busseto for eight years, learning and practicing on his battered little spinet (forerunner of the piano). It is still preserved today in the Milan Museum. There was Antonio Barezzi who became his second "father" and who helped the young Verdi in every way he could. In fact, his eight year old daughter, Margherita, would someday marry young Giuseppe! By 1823, he already was the organist of the village church in the tiny town of Le Roncole, only about three kilometers from Busseto.

It was here on October 12, 1813 that the boy was born who was destined to leave a musical heritage that has not been surpassed to the present time. The tiny farmhouse still stands not far from the beautiful villa that Verdi built—his beloved Sant'Agata. (We can go upstairs to see his small bedroom with its white, plastered walls and rough beams in the ceiling. A short walk brings us to the church where the ten year old played the organ for a small wage.) Very little seems to have changed from the days when Verdi walked from Busseto to Le Roncole to play the music of the Mass.

Fate certainly played a big part in shaping Giuseppe Verdi's life and therefore, his art. On May 4, 1836, at the age of twenty-three, he married his Margherita, also twenty-three. A year later their daughter Virginia was born. And in the next year their son Icilio arrived.

They were now living in Milan. Verdi was writing his first opera (*Oberto*). Suddenly tragedy struck. His daughter, barely seventeen months old, became ill and died on August 12, 1838. Fourteen months later on October 22, little Icilio followed. And, as if that was not enough, destiny struck again. The gentle Margherita, sickened with a brain inflammation, died June 18, nine months afterward. It was the year 1840. At the age of twenty-seven Verdi had lost his entire family.

How Verdi finally got over this shock will be told in later pages of this storybook. For now let's skip to the year 1862.

Verdi had been asked by the Imperial Theatre in Russia to write an opera. He had looked at several stories and finally chose one which he described as "a powerful drama...very vast...something out of the ordinary." It was a play written in 1835 by the Duke of Rivas, Don Angel of Saavedra, entitled *Don Alvaro* or the *Force of Destiny*. So Verdi's librettist Francesco Maria Piave set to work and so did Verdi. And on November 21, 1861 the composer wrote his publisher Tito Ricordi that the opera was finished. But it was not until almost a year later, November 10, 1862, that the premiere finally took place.

Let's imagine we're at the opera house in St. Petersburg, Russia—the place where Verdi's twenty-third opera was first performed. Soon we will hear and see how some people's lives are changed, shaped by... *The Force of Destiny* ... as the curtain is about to go up on...

5

La Forza Del Destino

(La FOR-tza dell Deh-STEE-no)

We have just heard the overture that began with six full chords. Then came the driving theme of the opera, followed by a sweet melody that tells us of the love of Donna Leonora and Don Alvaro. One beautiful tune follows another, *Forza* being one of the most melodious of Verdi's works and certainly one of the most melodious in all opera.

ACT I

The scene opens in a family room in the house of Vargas, Marquis of Calatrava (Cah-lah-TRAH-vah). The Marquis, Leonora's father, is saying goodnight to her, but notices that she is unhappy. He believes he has really broken up her love affair with someone he doesn't like.

However, Leonora is actually planning to elope that very night, even though she loves her father very much. Finally, Calatrava leaves. Curra (COO-rah), Leonora's maid, breathes with relief, "I thought he was going to stay till tomorrow!"

As Curra busily begins packing, Leonora tells her that she can't make up her mind about leaving; she loves her father and does not want to hurt him. However, Curra reminds her that her lover, Don Alvaro (Ahl-VAHR-oh), would probably be killed, or put in prison if her father found out. Of course, Leonora doesn't want to hear about this and tells Curra that she loves Alvaro so much that she's about to leave everything behind...father, country, and home.

Yet she hesitates. Suppose he doesn't come for her? It is already midnight. Just then the sound of horses is heard.

"He's here!"

"It was impossible that he would not come," says Curra.

But Leonora is torn. She wants to wait. In fact she wants to wait for tomorrow.

Alvaro is puzzled to say the least. He remarks that her hands are cold as death. He loses his temper, believing that Leonora does not love him after all. But Leonora does love him and tells him so in a lively aria... "I am yours, heart and soul...and I will follow you to the end of the earth!" Alvaro joins in.

They are almost at the balcony when suddenly a noise is heard. Someone is coming up the stairs!

"Quickly...we must go!" warns Leonora.

"It's too late!"

"Hide yourself!"

"No...I will defend you," declares Alvaro, taking out a pistol.

We hear the threatening, driving theme of the opera. With a crash, the door breaks open and the Marquis, sword in hand, rushes in followed by two servants. He is angry at the attempt to "seduce" his daughter! Leonora tries to hold him back.

"You are no longer my daughter!"

Don Alvaro dares him to strike him dead, but Calatrava scorns him saying that he is too low born. . .not worthy of being killed by a nobleman!

The Marquis orders his men to take Alvaro prisoner. But the Don once again takes out his pistol and forces the servants to leave. Then he tells Calatrava that he alone is guilty of the plan to elope, "Your daughter is as innocent as an angel. . . ." He will prove what he says by offering him his life. With this Don Alvaro throws his pistol to the floor! And here destiny takes over! As it hits the floor the gun goes off—and the bullet fatally wounds the Marquis!

With his dying breath, struggling to get the words out, he curses them both. And while the servants carry her father away, Leonora calls to heaven to forgive him. Her lover, desperate at the cruelty of fate, gently pulls Leonora to the balcony for their escape. The act ends.

ACT II

We are now at an inn located near the village of Hornachuelos. Dinner is being made in the large kitchen. The orchestra opens the scene with the same six deep chords of the first act. Peasants and muleteers are the customers. And there's a man who is supposed to be a student. It is really Don Carlo, Leonora's brother, in disguise. They ask him to give the supper blessing. Suddenly there is Leonora, dressed as a young man. She sees her brother and quickly hides once again.

Everybody is having a good time. There's lots of drinking and dancing. In comes a young gypsy girl who is greeted by all.

"Bravo...Preziosilla (Prez-ee-oh-SEE-ya)!" Don Carlo asks her to sit with him. Everyone wants their fortune told. Preziosilla asks them instead,

"Who wishes to *make* his fortune?"

"We all do!"

"Then hurry to Italy as soldiers and fight the Germans!"

"Death to the Germans!"

"They are the enemy of Italy and her sons!"

"We'll all go!"

"And I'll be with you," cries Preziosilla.

The drums start a military beat. The gypsy and chorus begin a quick tune..."In battle is glory!...You'll be a corporal...you'll be a colonel...!"

When the singing ends, Carlo asks the gypsy what will happen to a poor student. She looks at him and sadly tells him he is headed for misery. She doesn't hold out much hope for his future and then, in a low voice, tells him that he's not really a student but that his secret is safe with her. Then she once again takes up her carefree ways and tra-la-las away!

Outside a group of pilgrims pass by asking forgiveness from the Lord. All inside the inn now join them in solemn prayer. We see Leonora enter to pray. She asks the good Lord to protect her from her brother who wishes to kill her. Then she hides once more.

With the prayer ended, the "student" offers a toast to "this fine company." All are happy to join in. But Carlo has seen "a little person" who had arrived earlier with one of the muleteers named Trabuco.

"By the way," asks Carlo, "is it a rooster or a hen?" (man or woman?)

But Trabuco avoids the question. And, although Carlo tries to get the others to betray the mysterious youngster "who has no beard," he gets no answers. Finally, Trabuco tells him he's tired of all these questions and that he'd rather go to the stable to sleep with his mules! With that he picks up and leaves. Everyone laughs. But Carlo wants to play a trick—he wants to paint a mustache on the unknown "boy." Now the innkeeper objects. He has to protect his guests. "Instead, why don't you tell us who *you* are and where *you* are from?"

Carlo agrees and sings a melodious aria saying that his name is Pereda, a student with a bachelor's degree. Then he goes on to tell the story of his father's tragic "murder." He lies about his sister. He tells them that Leonora died with her father in the fight but that her "seducer" escaped. A friend (Vargas), swore to follow the killer, and right now this "friend" is crossing the ocean to America to catch him; while he, Pereda, is going back to his studies.

Well, everybody believes this tale but the gypsy girl. She lets him know that he hasn't fooled her one bit and with that she goes into her mocking tra-la-la as she did once before.

"It's late, my children," says the innkeeper, as he gets up. "Let's give thanks to the Lord and leave."

Everyone is tired and after a few farewells, they all leave for a good night's rest. We hear Preziosilla still laughing at the story that the "student" has just told. The scene slowly ends.

And so Don Carlo does not discover who the young stranger is. Leonora, for now, has escaped his hate. Although we never know why she and her lover parted, we just have to accept the "operatic" fact that they lost each other somehow, somewhere in their scramble to get away. When the curtains open once more, Leonora is near the church of the *Mother of the Angels*. It is night and the moon is very bright. A hooded figure silently makes its way to the heavy door. It is the beginning of the famous scene of the opera where the desperate Leonora seeks safety through the church. She is thankful that she has arrived without harm. She thinks that Don Alvaro left her and that he no longer loves her! So there is nothing else she can do. But this is a monastery. There's no place here for a woman! She cannot stand the thought that her lover has left her; all she has now is her faith in the Madonna. She sings a sweet prayer to our Lady, beginning: "Mother, Virgin Mother...forgive me..."

Then timidly, she gets to the big door. The driving theme music of the opera is heard again. Should she ring the bell at this late hour? Will they offer her someplace where she can be forever safe from her brother's dagger? "Don't forsake me, Lord, have pity on me now!" The full orchestra swells then slowly softens as the aria ends.

She rings the bell. Shortly, a small window in the door opens. The light shines in her face. A voice asks, "Who are you?"

"I wish to see the Superior...."

"The church opens at five in the morning...."

"The Superior...for pity's sake...!"

"What? At this hour?"

"Father Cleto sent me...."

Well, after a few more words, Friar Melitone (Mell-ee-TONE-eh) , who doesn't believe in much of what has been said, agrees to let the stranger inside.

"I can't come in!"

"No? Are you excommunicated (barred from the church)? Ah well, I'll announce you—and if I don't come back...good night!"

(Friar Melitone is one of those fussy, grumpy old fellows that gives us some chuckles, in contrast to the tragic story.)

The little window slaps shut. The opera's theme is heard again...followed by the beautiful melody of Leonora's earlier prayer. Suppose he refuses to see her? Suppose he tells her to go away? But he's supposed to be a merciful man. He'll protect her..."Holy Mother, help me...."

Soon the Superior, Father Guardiano (Gwar-dee-AH-no) appears followed by Friar (Brother) Melitone.

"Who wants me?"

"I do," whispers Leonora.

"Well...?"

"It's secret...."

"Leave us, Melitone...."

As the snoopy Brother leaves he is heard grumbling, "Always secrets...and only these "saints' know them...we're just nobodies...."

"Brother...are you grumbling?"

"Oh, no...I just said the door was heavy and noisy...."

And so Melitone shuffles off, still grumbling.

"Now we are alone," says Father Guardiano.

"I am a woman..."

"A woman at this hour! My Lord!"

Leonora, excited, tells him that she is "cursed by Heaven"— an unhappy woman who begs him to help her. She reminds him of Father Cleto's letter. Now he knows who she is...Leonora of Vargas! In a short, peaceful melody he asks her to approach the large stone cross that stands in the courtyard outside the church. Then, with the violins in the background, Leonora sings of the peace she now feels, while Guardiano joins in...telling her that the Lord will be merciful.

"Are you sure you want this life?"

"Yes."

Father Guardiano explains what he will do for her. She will be sent to a nearby cave where she will live alone. Only he will know who she is; only he will come to her each week to leave her food. Now the Father instructs Melitone to have all the brothers gather in front of the altar of the church. Leonora is grateful for her lonely hiding place. She thanks Father Guardiano, while he tells her that she will begin her secret life "at dawn."

"The good Lord will forgive me...," says Leonora.

Both sing the solemn duet, repeating these words as their voices reach the high note that ends their prayer. The scene comes to a close.

Before a high altar all the monks are standing holding lighted candles. The organ plays deep, opening music. Soon the violins are heard sweetly repeating the pleading theme of Leonora's prayer.

Now Guardiano begins to explain to all the friars that this "penitent soul" seeks shelter. No one is to go near the cave! They pledge to obey. The full chorus swells. "A thunderbolt" should strike anyone who dares to break this oath! All sing, with Leonora, a grand aria to the Virgin Mary asking her to protect this unlucky stranger...as Leonora leaves for the cave to begin a hermit's life. The curtain falls.

ACT III

We are now in Italy near the town of Villeteri. It is night; the woods are gloomy. We hear voices. Somewhere nearby some men are playing cards. As a figure slowly comes out of the woods, we hear a musical introduction.

The clarinet sings a sad, beautiful tune. We finally recognize Don Alvaro. He is now a captain in the Royal Spanish Grenadiers. He is also desperate. "Life is hell.... I wish I were dead...." He longs for Seville...for Leonora. He can hardly bear to think of that fateful night when destiny took away from him all that he had dreamed. He remembers how his father had battled to free his native land—the land of the Incas—from foreign rule! (Here Verdi is again telling his audience that Italy should free itself from Austrian rule.) But his father failed to become King of the Incas and instead was thrown into prison. There Alvaro was born, no one knowing that he was of royal birth.

"Ah, when will my misfortunes finally end?"

His thoughts again turn to his beloved Leonora. The sound of a delicate oboe begins. Alvaro, thinking that Leonora is dead, prays to her "who is among the angels" to help him get over his sorrows... "Oh, Leonora pity me...."

Suddenly, a fight is heard deep in the woods. There is a cry for help! Alvaro runs off. We hear the noise of a duel, the clashing of swords. In a moment Don Alvaro returns with (of all people) Don Carlo.

"They've run away. Are you hurt?"

"No...but I owe you my life."

"Who were they?"

"Frankly...it was a gambling fight...."

Carlo explains that he has just arrived with orders from the general... "and if it wasn't for you I'd be dead!"

The two men introduce themselves—but they each give a false name. When Carlo hears that he's been saved by the famous Captain Don Federico Herreros (alias Alvaro) he wants to be good friends... and they shake hands warmly.

A trumpet interrupts them. Voices shout a call to arms! And together in their new-found friendship the two men run off to join the battle.

When the curtains part again it is morning. We are in a small room in a house not far from the battleground. A military surgeon and some soldiers are at a window.

"Brave grenadiers!"

"Herreros is leading them!"

The surgeon, who has been looking through a telescope suddenly cries that Herreros is wounded and has fallen. His men are falling back! But wait, the Adjutant rallies the men and leads a charge! The Germans are running away—we've won! They're bringing in the captain... "wounded!" the soldiers exclaim. Outside voices are shouting.

"Glory to Spain!"

"Long live Italy!"

"We are victorious!"

In a moment Don Alvaro is carried in on a stretcher. The surgeon is on one side. Carlo, dusty from battle, sorrowfully walks on the other.

"Is he in danger?"

"I'm worried about the bullet in his chest."

Alvaro comes to slowly. "Where am I?" Carlo assures him that he is with friends and that the best care possible will save his life. Not only that, but he will be awarded the Order of Calatrava! At this Alvaro is startled and shudders. It is the name of the man he accidently killed! Although Don Carlo notices all this, he is still worried about his good friend. He asks the surgeon to leave them alone; Alvaro has something to say.

At this point there follows a duet that is probably the most moving ever written for two men, tenor and baritone. It begins with Don Alvaro's words, sung softly... "In this solemn hour... swear that you are my devoted friend...."

"I swear it...I swear it...."

Alvaro tells Carlo that he has a key in his breast pocket along with a sealed, faded letter. He will trust Carlo to burn it after his death.

"I swear it will be done...."

"Then...I will die in peace...."

"My friend...put your faith in Heaven...."

And with Alvaro repeating that now at last he will be at peace knowing that his dying wish will be kept...while Carlo tries to comfort him...the moving duet ends..."farewell...farewell...."

They gently carry the wounded man away to be cared for by the surgeon. Don Carlo begins to wonder. Why did his dying friend shudder at the name of Calatrava? Could it be that he is his enemy...the seducer of his sister, Leonora... the murderer of his father? The key he was given will open the secret! He takes out some papers from Alvaro's packet. As he is about to open them he is stopped by his conscience. "What am I doing? I swore an oath...*and* he saved my life!"

Carlo fights to keep from opening the secret papers. Finally he decides to keep his oath of honor. But, he thinks, maybe there are some other things that will give him an answer! He looks once again inside the bag. A portrait! It's not sealed...and it wasn't mentioned. In a second he opens the case and there's Leonora's picture! So...it *is* Alvaro! Carlo is enraged—"Let him live so that he may die at my hands!"

The surgeon enters. Yes, Alvaro will live—here is the bullet. Don Carlo is overjoyed. At last he has found his enemy! He will die by his sword and then he will find Leonora and she shall follow her lover to the place of the damned. The scene ends.

When the curtains part once more, we are at an army camp near Villeteri. It is night. No one is in sight.

> *Before we continue the story let's talk about cuts in opera. That is, skipping parts of what the composer originally put down. Through the years, for reasons best known to the people who have put on the operas, certain scenes and music have disappeared from the stage. Then others have put them back in...and so on. In this opera the following meeting between Carlo and Alvaro is sometimes left out. So, if you don't hear it on some records, or at some performances, just blame whoever left it out years ago. For us, it will make the story stick together better if we go back to what Verdi and his librettist, Francesco Maria Piave, actually wrote.*

Dawn is not far off. The night guards come in and sing a short chorus. They're looking over the camp to be sure everything is safe. Then they quietly leave again, saying that soon the morning call will wake everybody up for the day.

Don Alvaro, now fully recovered from his wound, walks in. He's still thinking of the tragedy of the accidental shooting, of Leonora who he believes is probably dead...and of his own destiny. He just can't seem to get peace of mind.

Carlo comes in and calls to him. Alvaro turns and goes gladly to greet his friend who helped save his life.

"Has your wound healed?"

"Yes...."

"Could you fight a duel?"

"I don't understand...."

"Oh, no? Don Alvaro—the *Indian!*"

Don Alvaro is shocked to think that Carlo has broken his vow about reading his letters. But Carlo tells him he didn't have to...he saw Leonora's picture! We hear the old bitterness opening up again. Alvaro discovers something he didn't know—Leonora is alive! But Don Carlo tells him she is destined to die because he himself has sworn to kill her! Not if Don Alvaro can help it! Swords are drawn and the two enemies begin a duel. In come the guards.

"Hold it! Stop!"

"Drag him away!"

The guards drag Carlo away as he calls out, "Murderer of my father!" Alvaro stands there still holding his sword. What shall he do? How will he ever find peace? Then he gets an idea. He will find his peace of mind in a monastery! He throws down his sword and takes off.

(Why anyone ever decided to leave out this important scene is a mystery.) Anyway, in a moment...with the coming of daybreak...drums roll and trumpets blare, and the camp comes to life. Soldiers sing of their life of fun and adventure...who cares what tomorrow will bring? Preziosilla asks the women of the camp to gather around and she will tell them their fortunes. Soon everybody is having a good time. Wine-sellers give them drinks.

"To our health!"

"Hurrah!"

"To Spain! To a united Italy!"

"To our hero...Don Federico Herreros!"

"And to his noble friend...!"

Trabuco, the peddler, comes in whining about who will buy his wares..."I buy and sell anything...."

The soldiers fall for his "bargains" and soon there's a lively scene where each is trying to cheat the other. In the long run, Trabuco makes out very well and continues on his way.

Now, to the sound of sad voices, we see some peasants begging for bread. At the same time we hear the young voices of some new soldier boys who are very homesick.

Then, getting back to a light, cheerful tune, the wine-sellers offer the boys some drinks...to "comfort" them.

Preziosilla takes a couple of them by the arms. "Shame on you...are you babies...are you crazy?" She tells them to look around and they'll surely find someone who'll take their minds off home!

Everybody joins in..."let's have fun...and forget everything else!" (All through this scene, as with the whole opera, there is one wonderful melody after another, weaving in and out— tempting us to hum along.) Finally, the women wine-sellers grab some of the young soldiers and dance a lively *tarantella* (a fun folk-dance). Onto this scene enters fat Friar Melitone! He's soon caught up in the dance and is whirled around whether he likes it or not. When he finally gets loose he goes into a long story about what a "wild life" these people are leading. He complains that he came from Spain to heal wounds and to cure souls...and instead he sees people making merry on Sunday...drinking...flirting—"you all play tricks with Venus (goddess of love) and Bacchus (god of wine)!"

Soon the Italian soldiers are fed up with his complaining and want to hit him on the head. The Spanish soldiers try to protect him. But nothing seems to help until Preziosilla decides the one way to get the soldiers' attention is to start beating a drum! This does the trick and soon they're all singing in imitation of the sounds of drums!

"Ra-ta-plan, Ra-ta-plan...sounds of glory..."

"Pim, pum, pum...victory wins every soldier's heart!"

And with everybody singing at the top of their lungs, while Melitone finally makes his escape, the act ends.

ACT IV

At the *Mother of Angels,* a sorry group of beggars holding bowls or plates or cups is asking for food. We see Melitone with a large pot of soup. "What do you take this for—a hotel?" But the women and old men press forward to get their share of the soup.

"Fill up four for me...."

"Four for her!"

"Four for her!"

"Yes...because I have six children to feed...."

"Why have you got six?" asks Melitone.

"Because that's what God sent me...."

"Oh, sure, sure...God sent them. Well, you wouldn't have them if you spent the night saying your rosary..."

Father Guardiano, who has entered the area, now tells Friar Melitone to be more merciful.

"Father Raffaello is more kind...," call the women.

"He is an angel. . . ."

"A saint!"

Well, this makes Melitone finally lose his temper and in a fit he chases them all away.

"Oof, I haven't any more patience," cries Friar Melitone.

"Well, the good Lord didn't give you too much," says Guardiano, "giving charity. . . would make an angel happy."

"An angel wouldn't last three days in my place," answers Melitone.

"Quiet. . . even though you're bothered because they all would rather have Friar Raffaello!"

Melitone protests that Friar Raffaello is really his friend but that he does have a pair of eyes that scare him sometimes. The other day he was so surprised by Raffaello's bulging eyes that he told him he looked like a half-breed, like a wild Indian!

The bell rings. Father Guardiano tells Melitone to go open the door, and then leaves.

It is Don Carlo! He asks for a Father Raffaello. There are two of them, comments Melitone—one is fat and deaf as a post, the other is thin with dark eyes (Lord, what eyes!). So Don Carlo, follows Melitone inside. And there's Friar Raffaello—alias Don Alvaro! Carlo scornfully tells him that he's been searching for him for five years and has found him at last—dressed in a hypocrite's costume! Now he has come to avenge his honor! Don Alvaro is stunned. He explains that he has tried to lose himself—and his past—by becoming a monk. He pleads with Don Carlo to leave him in peace! But Carlo will have none of this.

"You are a coward. . . but nothing will protect you from me!"

Alvaro can hardly hold himself back, but in a lovely aria (introduced by a soulful oboe) he continues to ask for pardon. . . for mercy. But Don Carlo, using the same melody, repeats the story of Alvaro's "crime". . . and vows to kill him.

Still trying to get Don Carlo to understand that he did not murder his father or seduce Leonora, Don Alvaro, in a very gentle melody, insists that...

"I love her still..."

"You can't appease my anger with your lying words...."

"Look then,...I beg you on my knees...."

"That just proves that you are nothing better than a base half-breed!"

Half-breed! Now Alvaro can no longer hold his temper! With a glorious high note he finally asks to be given a sword! Carlo is overjoyed and with a long, full-voiced note in return he sings out the word..."Finally!" But once again the strains of the oboe are heard and once again Alvaro gets hold of himself and tells him that the devil will *not* win!

"Go...away...."

"Are you trying to make a fool out of me? Well, if you're too much of a coward to fight...then I'll disgrace you with this!"

Carlo strikes Alvaro across the face! At last Alvaro loses his head. Picking up the sword they rush off to duel to the death! The scene ends.

The next scene shows us the spot where Leonora has been hiding. Night is beginning to fall; the moon rises. From the cave a figure appears. It is the pale, unhappy girl who has chosen to be a hermit...away from the world forever. We hear the orchestra once again playing the familiar, driving "destiny" music. Suddenly, in a burst of sadness Leonora sings one of the most beautiful arias ever written—one that every dramatic soprano loves to sing because of its beauty as well as its difficulty. To a light harp accompaniment Leonora cries out...in one long, moving note...the word:

"Peace—peace my God...I suffer as much today—all through the years—as I suffered that first unfortunate

day...I loved him...and I still do...though I shall not see
him again...O Lord, let me die...for peace will only come
from death...."

Then on a high, dramatic note Leonora realizes that peace will
never come...and that she will suffer forever! She goes to where
her food has been left by Father Guardiano. We hear the mood
of the music change. Someone is coming.

"Who goes there? Who dares to enter this sacred spot?
A curse on you!"

And with a blood-tingling "high C"...she runs to the cave
and quickly closes the heavy wooden door.

The duel is taking place. Offstage we hear the beating of
swords and in a moment the voice of Don Carlo.

"I am dying...I wish to confess...to save my soul!"

Don Alvaro rushes into the scene. He carries a bloody sword.
Once again he has spilled the blood of a Vargas! He runs to the
cave and calls for the "hermit" to come out to help save a dying man.

"I cannot!"

"Brother...in the name of the Lord!"

But Leonora is panicked. She rings the bell over her door to
call for help against this stranger. Finally, she appears at the doorway and demands that he run from the wrath of heaven. All at
once the two lovers recognize each other. Alvaro thinks he sees
a ghost! But no...it is really Leonora...it is truly Alvaro.

"Stay away from me...my hands are stained with
blood...."

Alvaro tells her that he tried not to fight but was forced into
it and now—out there—lies a man dying.

"Who is he?"

"Your brother...!"

"Good God...!"

Leonora rushes off to the wounded man, while Alvaro desperately curses destiny for this latest agony. He has once again found his love...and he meets her with her brother's blood on his hands!

We hear a scream! The orchestra crashes repeatedly. Leonora now appears held up by Father Guardiano. She is wounded...Her brother finally made good his threat to kill her—she is stabbed and dying.

All three now raise their voices, Alvaro recalling the curse...Guardiano telling him not to be sacrilegious while this angel, Leonora, is soon to fly to God's heavenly throne.

And Leonora, with her dying breath, tells Alvaro that she pardons him. Heaven will forgive him through her. In a slow, lovely melody she tells him that at last she will find peace. Alvaro sadly realizes that he alone, "the guilty one," will remain unpunished.

And now to the quivering sound of violins...Leonora voices her dying words...

"Oh, heaven, I'm waiting for you...goodbye, Alvaro...I shall await you there...!"

"Dead!" cries Alvaro.

"She has risen to heaven," reminds Father Guardiano.

As the music and voices fade...the orchestra plays the last, repeated chords.

THE CURTAIN FALLS

And with the close of this most melodious opera we are reminded that Giuseppe Verdi certainly knew how cruel fate can be. Perhaps the words "She has risen to heaven," reminded Verdi once again of his beloved Margherita who died so young...over twenty years ago.

He had sworn never to write music again. What happened to

change his mind? It was years later that Verdi himself told the story.

It seems that the head of the opera house in Milan—the famous La Scala—ran into the unhappy young man and, walking arm in arm in the snow, told him about a wonderful new libretto about Nebuchadnezzar, the king of ancient Babylon (*Nabucco*).

Bartolomeo Merelli urged him to take it and read it. "What good is it to me?" asked Verdi, "I don't want to read any librettos." But Merelli insisted so Verdi stuck it in his pocket and took it home. When he arrived he threw the play on his table. (And here, once again, fate had its way.) The libretto actually opened on the page that had these words: *Va, pensiero, sull'ali dorate,* "Go thoughts... on golden wings." Soon he was reading one part, then another and another. When he returned the booklet to Merelli the next day, he had to admit that it was excellent... but that he would not *think* of writing an opera. Once again Merelli forced Verdi to take it home. And so, in Verdi's own words... "one day, one line... one day another... now a note... now a phrase"—slowly, slowly Verdi was writing again!

How lucky for us that destiny and Merelli pulled the strings. How lucky that Verdi's own nature, his deep sense of patriotism and love of Italy took hold. Here he again had the chance— through *Nabucco*—to tell the people of Italy to rise and free themselves from the rule of Austria! For in the famous chorus already mentioned, where the Hebrews sing of their yearning to be free of Babylon and to find the promised land, Italians could hear their own voices raised in their call for freedom!

And so the morning after the premier of *Nabucco* at La Scala, March 9, 1842, Verdi was famous throughout the city. That deeply moving chorus was being sung everywhere... soon to become the underground national anthem of Italy! On the walls of the city the words "Viva Verdi" appeared; "Long live Verdi!" And soon the name Verdi not only stood for the heroic composer but took on a deeper meaning. It became an acronym—each letter beginning a word that leads to a full slogan:

"*Vittorio Emmanuele Re D'Italia*"—Victor Emmanuel King of Italy!

And eighteen years later—in 1860—Victor Emmanuel did indeed become the first King of Italy!

Giuseppe Verdi had come into his own. Opera after opera poured out—twenty-six in all—filling the world with music that has lived for over one hundred years... music that will continue to touch our hearts, our emotions, for countless years to come.

But now where shall we go? We certainly don't want to leave the opera house and Verdi's immortal music of *La Forza del Destino*... with its grand medieval settings. We've certainly come to know Seville pretty well. Why not continue with Verdi and see where he could take us next? We could travel just north of Spain through tiny villages, peaceful countryside... until we arrive into the bustling city, the beautiful city of Paris. Let's go!

Paris, the "City of Light," had been host to Verdi and his friend Giuseppina Strepponi during the winter of 1851-1852 while he was writing one of his greatest operas, *Il Trovatore* (The Troubador). This was to be performed for the first time in January of 1853 at the Apollo Theatre in Rome. But he also had scheduled the opening of another new opera for March of the same year! (By the time he got to Rome he was rehearsing one during the day and writing music for the other at night!) And what was the other opera he was working on? None other than *La Traviata* (Lah Trah-vee-AH-tah)! During that winter in Paris he saw a play Alexander Dumas Jr. had written from Dumas' own book, *La Dame aux Camellias*, "The Lady of the Camellias." Verdi was so taken with this story that by the time he had arrived in Rome, he already had *La Traviata* (The Lost One) in the works.

But Paris is where we are now and Paris is where *La Traviata* lives so let's once more go to the opera house to hear a kind of work that Verdi was never to write again!

Up till now (and afterwards), Verdi's settings were vast, about characters of a different time and place. *Traviata* is about people of his own time; it is intimate, it flows right along with one thing leading to another without skipping around. And it's about a real girl who made a name for herself by not being too careful about her morals! However, unlike Carmen, she traveled in high society (but one that the *true* society people did not approve of). Dumas gave it a name—the demi-mond—or the "half-society," a group that was only *half* recognized.

So Verdi not only wrote an opera "of today," but one about a type of person who was thought "sensational." In the book she was named Marguerite Gautier. In real life she was named Rose Alphonsine Plessis, but she changed her name to Marie Duplessis when, as a teenager, she began to enter the demi-mond. And in the opera we meet her as Violetta Valery!

The curtain is about to rise on the story of the "lost one"— the girl who lived for each moment—who did not want to fall in love, but did...the story of...

6

La Traviata

(Lah Trah-vee-AH-tah)

Before we enter Violetta's world we hear the orchestra. The soft sounds of thin violins swell into a sweeping melody that we will hear later when Violetta thinks of her Alfredo. Soon the violins begin to go silent. There is a pause. Then with a great burst, the full orchestra announces the scene of a party taking place in Violetta's house.

ACT I

The curtain quickly goes up to show a rich salon with Violetta and her friends having a good time.

There are the usual latecomers. Of course Flora Bervoix (Bare-VWAH) is one of them, along with the Marquis D'Obigny (Dobe-en-YEE) and the Baron Douphol (Doo-FOLE).

"You're late...," says Violetta.

"We were gambling at Flora's...and the time just flew...."

"Flora, and friends...let's have some more fun with what's left of the night...."

Meanwhile, behind all this, the orchestra is playing a brilliant, lively melody that mirrors the cheerfulness of the party.

"Yes,...life is made for pleasure!"

While all this is going on two young gentlemen enter and go over to Violetta. One is her friend the Viscount Gaston de Letorieres (Let-or-ee-AIR). With him is a stranger.

"Here is another who thinks highly of you, my lady... Alfredo Germont (Jerh-MONE)...."

Violetta, with great charm, offers Germont her hand and he gallantly kisses it.

Dinner is about to be served. Everything is ready. Violetta asks her guests to go and be seated.

Privately, Gaston mentions to Violetta that his friend Alfredo is always thinking about her.

"You're joking...!"

But Gaston tells her that Alfredo was around her home every day when she was sick.

"Stop it...I am nothing to him...."

Gaston insists that he is telling her the truth. And Alfredo, with a sigh, tells her that it is really so. Violetta of course is puzzled but pleased, although she tries to brush the whole thing off. Meanwhile the Baron, who is Violetta's present friend, tells Flora that he doesn't like that young man.

Well, the small talk goes on, with Alfredo paying close attention to the girl he loves. Then the guests suddenly ask the Baron for a toast. He refuses. So Gaston asks his friend to do the honors. But Alfredo tells him that he isn't quite in the mood. However Gaston asks him again and soon everybody is calling on Alfredo to give a toast.

"Would you like that?" asks Alfredo, turning to Violetta.

"Yes...."

Let's listen to the "singer!" Here Alfredo sings the famous drinking song of the opera. It is in waltz time and he soon directs it to Violetta as he speaks of love. All join in. Then Violetta, using the same melody, rises to say that her joy is being with all her friends.

"Let us be happy! For the happiness of love soon disappears...it is a flower that is born, then dies, never to be enjoyed again...." (Remember Juliet?)

And so, with all the guests adding their voices, the delightful, swaying, drinking song ends.

But the music continues and over it we hear Violetta telling Alfredo that the only thing worthwhile in life is having fun.

"Only when someone is not yet in love," says Alfredo.

Once again the merry-makers come back to the drinking song, all ending in a high, extended note.

Then there is another sound of music. It is the signal for a dance. Everyone loves the idea and they begin to leave for the next room, when suddenly Violetta gives a cry. She is feeling faint!

"What is it?" they ask in alarm.

"Nothing..."

Violetta tries to go on but she can't. They help her to a sofa. Everyone, especially Alfredo, is now very worried but Violetta tells them to go inside and that she will join them soon. They slowly do so except for Alfredo. Violetta doesn't see him. She

painfully goes to a mirror and is surprised at how pale she looks.
As she turns, there's Alfredo!

"Has the pain gone away?"

"I feel better...."

He warns her that she is leading the kind of life that could kill
her and that she should take better care of herself.

"Is it possible?"

"If you were mine...I'd look after you...."

Violetta can hardly believe that there might be someone who
really cares for her. Alfredo instead, cannot believe that no one
in the world really loves her.

"No one..."
"Except me..."

At this Violetta laughs and somewhat sarcastically says that
she had forgotten about "his great love for me."

Alfredo is hurt by her laughter and insists that he really, truly
loves her. Violetta begins to reflect. Could it really be?

"Have you been in love with me for long?"

"Oh, yes...for a whole year!"

Slowly the music introduces a tender love song in which Alfredo
tells Violetta that from that "one happy day" when he first saw
her he has been secretly in love...a love so deep that it has
been pain and delight...that mysterious feeling that comes from
the heart.

But the young Violetta answers him in a light, frivolous—almost
laughing—tune telling him that if he truly loves her then it would
be better if he runs from her.

"True friendship I can offer you...but I don't know what
love is...so find someone else to love...that way you
won't find it hard to forget me...."

But Alfredo continues with his longing love song...and soon
Violetta joins in with the same melody—but insisting that he

should forget all about her.

In the middle of it all Gaston appears.

"What the devil are you two doing...?"

"Just having fun...," says Violetta.

"Ah-hah...that's good...stay right where you are!"

And Gaston leaves once more. Now Violetta, still afraid of any serious attachment to anyone, asks Alfredo to speak no more of love. Alfredo is hurt and so without argument he tells her that he will do as she wishes. Much to her surprise he is going to leave altogether! Still not sure of her feelings, and to soften the blow to Alfredo, she takes a flower from her dress and offers it to him. It is a camellia. (Remember how Carmen did the same thing? Only, you will recall that it was quite different. She threw the flower—a rose—at Jose's feet and turned seductively away.)

But Violetta holds out the flower to him.

"Take this flower..."

"Why?"

"So that you can bring it back..."

"When?" asks Alfredo, turning in wonder.

"When it is faded," she replies quietly.

Alfredo realizes what she is really saying! It means that he can see her again tomorrow!

"All right then...tomorrow," whispers Violetta with a smile.

At this, of course, Alfredo is overjoyed.

"Do you still say that you love me?" asks Violetta, who wants to believe it herself.

"Oh...I love you so very much!"

Alfredo again starts to leave, but comes back to kiss her hand, as together they sing "goodbye...."

Now the rest of the party starts to return from their dance.

They, too, go to Violetta to say goodbye. In a lively chorus they sing of the dawn arriving and to thank her for a wonderful time. The voices rise to a climax as the guests gradually leave.

Violetta is now alone. She cannot forget what has happened to her this night. It's strange...the effect that young man has had on her....She begins to sing a fantastic aria in three parts that is one of the greatest that Verdi (or anyone else) ever wrote. Here there must be a voice that is more than one voice. Dramatic soprano, lyric soprano, *coloratura* soprano: powerful, yet heavenly, beautiful and full of the ability to fly from note to note with the grace of a bird.

> "It's strange...it's strange...I cannot forget his words...Would true love really be bad for me? Oh joy that I do not know...to love and to be loved.... Can I forsake it...for the empty follies of my present life?"

Then she repeats the music that Alfredo first sang to her... about a love so deep that it is pain and delight...that mysterious feeling that comes from the heart.

Violetta is now deep in these thoughts of love. But then she tries to take hold of herself and with a ringing tone she cries...

> "This is folly! Folly!...useless thinking! Here I am alone...in this populated desert that's called Paris! What can I hope for?"

Then in a shower of colorful notes she states that all she can do is enjoy herself...and die in the attempt! She laughs at the thought, and now, really convinced, she throws herself into the final part of the aria...

> "I must be forever free. I will fly from one joy to another...From dawn to dusk...I will always seek new happiness...!"

But Violetta has never met anyone like Alfredo, for, right in the middle of her saying that she must remain forever free...she hears his voice once again. He has not yet left her as he sings (from outdoors) the same words that he sang to her when he first told her of his love.

"Love...mysterious love...that is both pain and joy to one's heart..."

And so while Alfredo repeats his love for Violetta, she still sings of...

"ever new delights...that will be her only thoughts..."

The act ends.

ACT II

To some excited music the scene opens on the garden of a country house in a suburb of Paris called Auteuil. Three months have gone by. Alfredo walks in dressed in riding clothes (Verdi wanted him in hunting clothes, but...). Anyway, he is full of happiness; he and Violetta have been living in paradise and are very much in love. The rest of the world is far away. Violetta lives for him alone...and he for her. His bubbling nature and his youthful passion have grown into a peaceful love because her gentle smile tells him she lives for him alone.

As Alfredo's singing ends we hear hurried music and in comes Violetta's maid Annina. She is in traveling clothes so Alfredo wants to know where she's been.

"I come from Paris."

As Alfredo questions her further we learn (and much to his surprise) that she had been sent to sell Violetta's horses, carriages—in fact, everything she owns. Alfredo is stunned.

"It's a big expense for you both to live here," reminds Annina.

"How much is needed?"

"A thousand louis!" (About six thousand dollars.)

Alfredo asks Annina not to say anything to Violetta but that he will go at once to Paris and take care of the bills. Just as he leaves, Violetta walks in with a handful of papers. She's been the one who has taken care of the finances. And right now, she's waiting for her business manager to see where things stand.

"Where's Alfredo?"

"He's just left for Paris."

"When will he return?"

"Before nightfall..."

"That's strange..."

But before she has any more time to think about this, her servant, Giuseppe, comes in and hands her a letter. Violetta reminds him that she's expecting a businessman and tells Giuseppe to let him in at once.

When she opens the letter she laughingly finds that her friend, Flora, has discovered her hiding place and has invited her to a ball...for that very night. But Violetta has another life now—she's found true love—and so she tosses the invitation on the table. Flora will not see *her!*

In a moment Giuseppe comes back to tell her that a gentleman is waiting. Violetta thinks it's the accountant, but the dark notes of the orchestra tells us that it is...Alfredo's father, Giorgio Germont!

Violetta is astonished...and when the old man starts in by accusing her of ruining his son, she tells him that she is a lady and that she will not go on with this conversation.

Germont is surprised and impressed with her manner. But he then suggests that Alfredo will give her everything he owns.

"He wouldn't dare...I would refuse!"

"But what about all this luxury...?"

Violetta simply hands him her papers. With just a glance he discovers that Violetta, in fact, is the one who has been paying all the bills. Yet the old man is troubled. He soon calls on Violetta's good nature to make a sacrifice. She's frightened and afraid to hear more.

"I want to assure the future of my two children...."

"*Two* children...?"

To Violetta's surprise Germont tells her that Alfredo has a sister, a young and beautiful girl, about to be married. And if it is known that her brother is having an affair, her fiancé would leave her! (How times have changed!)

"Oh, you want me to stay away from Alfredo for awhile..."

"That's not what I want..."

"I'm offering quite a lot..."

"But not enough..."

Violetta is shocked. She knows now that Germont wants her to give up Alfredo forever! At this the orchestra crashes... then in short, excited notes Violetta tells him of how great a love she has for his son.

"Don't you know that I have no one in this world but Alfredo...don't you know that I have a fatal sickness? I already see the end of my life! I would rather die...than be away from Alfredo!"

Her voice rises and in a long, desperate note her pleading ends. Germont knows that she is being asked to make a great sacrifice...but she is young...and perhaps in time...

"It is impossible...he is the only one I want to love!"

But then in short, solid notes Germont reminds her that men are fickle. What will happen when her beauty fades? And how can he, Germont, or any parent...agree to a son living like this?

Violetta begins to admit to herself that this is true. Germont asks her again to give up this fragile dream and become "the guardian angel of my family...." He pleads with her to understand him.

Violetta is torn apart. She sees now that hope is dead and in a sweeping melody she tells of her defeat, while Germont still begs her to be a guardian angel.

Now she is finally in tears. With a long sighing note she begins a sweet, low melody asking him to tell his daughter... "that lovely and pure young girl," that Violetta gave up her one hope for a good life for her.

"Sacrificed it for her...and I now will die...die... die...."

Both join in a melodious duet. She asks that he tell his daughter about her sacrifice, while he (more and more impressed with her goodness) admits that he, too, is now suffering with her...and that she should try to have courage in all that she is doing. Violetta now takes hold of her feelings.

"Now...tell me what to do."

"Tell him you don't love him anymore..."

"He won't believe me..."

"Leave him..."

"He'll follow me..."

Finally, Violetta has a plan but will not tell Germont what it is since he would not want her to do it. She asks him to embrace her as a daughter. To hurried music, the old man asks what she would like him to do for her. Violetta simply repeats that she will die...but that she wishes that someone will tell Alfredo of her great suffering and sacrifice. The sorrowful duet builds to a climax with Germont assuring her that she will one day be proud of her noble action.

She hears someone coming.

"Leave me...we will probably never meet again!"

And, while she once again pleads with him to tell Alfredo of her reason for leaving, they sing their "goodbyes" as the orchestra ends with five stirring chords.

Violetta now goes into action. She writes a short reply to Flora that she will come to the party. She rings for Annina who is surprised at the address.

"Quiet! Go deliver this at once!"

Now she must write a farewell note to Alfredo. We hear the "crying" of the oboe as she wonders what to tell him. Finally she seals the letter. And not a moment too soon, since Alfredo comes in and asks what she is doing. She tries to hide the letter; she's confused. Luckily Alfredo is thinking about other things, so when she refuses to give him the letter he lets the matter go. He's worried about getting a visit from his father who wrote him a strong note. But he assures Violetta...

"...he'll love you at first sight...."

"I don't want him to find me here...."

Trying not to show that she has been crying, Violetta tells him that she's sure that his father will let them stay together and that they will be happy forever after. Then, almost desperate, she asks him to tell her that he loves her.

"I love you so much...why are you crying?"

"I had to...now I feel better...."

She will be in the garden, near to him—always near to him. And then, unable to control herself, she sweeps into a beautiful melody asking him to always love her. (It is the same music that we heard in the prelude—before Violetta's party.)

"Love me, Alfredo...love me as much as I love you...goodbye...."

And to quick, excited music she runs into the garden.

Alfredo, now alone, wonders if his father will come at all since it is already quite late. Giuseppe enters to tell him that the lady of the house has left...a carriage was waiting for her. She is now on her way to Paris, where Annina has already gone.

Alfredo, of course, believes that this trip is only to help pay the bills. Violetta will try to sell all she owns, but Annina will stop her.

He has hardly thought about all this when a messenger enters with a letter from "the lady who just left in a carriage." Alfredo is surprised and begins to get upset. What could this be? Why is he feeling so shaken? He finally finds the courage to open the note. He has just barely begun to read the first few words...

"Alfredo, by the time you receive this message..."

...when he realizes what has happened! Violetta has left him!

As he turns in sorrow he is suddenly face to face with his father and with a cry of despair he falls into his arms.

The unhappy old man knows how much his son is suffering. He tries to help him. But Alfredo is full of grief.

The orchestra now begins an introduction to one of the finest baritone arias in opera. Germont asks...

"Who made you forget the seas and the land of your home in Provence...? Remember how happy you were there...Ah, you don't know how much your old father has suffered...May God grant that you will return...."

But Alfredo is torn with anger. He wants vengeance! It's that Baron Douphol...who has taken Violetta away from him!

No, he will not return home with his father! Suddenly he finds Flora's invitation. That's all he needs to convince him. Violetta has gone to the ball. So he will go there to get his revenge! Alfredo rushes out, while his father follows to try to stop him.

And to the sound of seven heavy chords the scene comes to a fearful end.

To the lively action of violins the next scene opens in Flora's house. It's a richly furnished place with bright lighting. Flora comes in with the Marquis, Doctor Grenville and the other guests invited to this masquerade party.

"We'll have a good time at tonight's masquerade," says Flora. "I've even invited Violetta and Alfredo...."

"Haven't you heard? They've separated!"

Flora and the doctor are shocked. But before they can say anything, some of the women guests, dressed as Spanish gypsies, dance in. As they sing and dance, with tambourines keeping time, the orchestra begins a lively waltz that reminds us of a tune we heard in the first act. As the "gypsies" sway to the colorful melody, they pretend to read Flora's palm...then the Marquis'.

"Let's see...you, lady, have many rivals...."

"Marquis...you're not a model of faithfulness...."

Flora tells the Marquis (who is supposed to be *her* companion) that he'd better be careful. The Marquis objects that the story isn't true, but Flora tells him that a wolf may be able to change clothes, but he is still a wolf!

To a swirling, swaying dance the chorus now sings that what is past is past. In a moment the orchestra introduces the men, led by Gaston, dressed as Spanish matadors and picadors.

"We're the Matadors of Madrid...just arrived in Paris...

Listen to our story—it will tell you the kind of lovers we are...!"

And so to a lively *cabaletta* they tell the story of Piquillo. He's a matador who's been told by the girl he loves that he has to kill *five bulls in one day* in order to win her! So he goes about doing just that—and wins the girl.

After some "bravos" from the ladies and an answer from the "matadors," all call for the gambling to begin!

Suddenly Alfredo comes in. Everyone is startled to see him there—and without Violetta. He doesn't know where she is.

"So now you're free! Good! Let's start gambling!"

The orchestra, led by violins, begins with a low, threatening sound. Violetta arrives with the Baron!

He sees Alfredo at once and warns Violetta not to say a word to that "common one." Violetta is already sorry that she came.

Meanwhile, Alfredo can't lose. He wins hand after hand. Lucky at cards, unlucky in love! Yes, he'll be a winner tonight and then he'll return to the country.

"Alone?" asks Flora.

"No, no. . .with the one who was with me. . .and then ran away from me. . .!"

Violetta hears him in despair. Gaston asks him to have pity on her.

We see that the Baron wants to join the gambling—against Alfredo. (In the background there's the waltz melody from Act I.)

Violetta, to herself, sings a gliding little tune in which she wonders what will happen, praying that the Lord will have pity on her.

Again, Alfredo wins. In two turns of the cards he has won from the Baron three hundred louis (about eighteen hundred dollars)!

"Want to keep going?" asks Alfredo.

But before the Baron can answer, a servant announces that supper is served. Everyone begins to leave for dinner. Again we hear Violetta sing that same sweeping melody. . .as she, too, leaves.

Only the Baron and Alfredo remain.

"Want to go on?"

"We can't now. . .but later I'll win it back. . . ."

The two rivals leave. Again the orchestra sounds deeply. Then to hurried music, Violetta comes back. She is soon followed by Alfredo.

"You called for me?" asks Alfredo, coldly.

"You must leave. . .you're in danger. . . ."

"Oh, I get it! Stop it! Do you think I'm so bad. . .?"

"No, no. . .never. . .!"

"Well then, what scares you. . .?"

"I'm always afraid of the Baron."

Alfredo, angrily singing to a somewhat marching rhythm, asks if she's afraid that he'll kill the Baron who is both "her lover and her protector!" But Violetta sadly tells him that she would die if he, Alfredo, would be lost in a duel.

"What do you care?"

"Please go at once!"

"I'll go...but you must swear that you'll follow me...."

"Ah, no, never...!"

"Never?"

Violetta, almost breathlessly, pleads with him to leave...that she has sworn a sacred oath to run from him! Alfredo demands to know who forced her to swear. It was Douphol, wasn't it? Violetta is forced to lie.

"Then you love him?"

"All right...I love him...."

Alfredo loses his head. He calls out to all the guests to come back into the room.

"You all know this woman?"

"Who? Violetta?"

"Don't you know what she has done?"

"No!"

Violetta is horrified and in tears. A full chord begins Alfredo's passionate and sarcastic story.

This woman, Violetta, gave him everything because she said she loved him. He, the blind fool, let her. But now he wants to make up for that. "So you all are witnesses that I have paid her back!" With this angry shout, Alfredo throws the money he has just won at Violetta's feet!

Everyone is shocked at this terrible act—and in accusing voices, tell Alfredo to leave at once!

Before he can move, his father appears! He has seen everything and in a sad melody tells Alfredo that he who insults a woman is no longer his son. Alfredo feels miserable at what he has done.

Everyone pities poor Violetta. They try to stop her from crying. The Baron is about to challenge Alfredo to a duel. Although Germont knows how much Violetta really loves his son, he must keep the secret. And then, as all these different thoughts blend, Violetta, in a lovely, touching melody, sings of how much she loves Alfredo.

"Ah, even when I am gone...I shall love you still...!"

All these emotions—a dozen different musical ideas—come together in a typical Verdi climax of sound that fills us with its passion and power!

Baron Douphol angrily throws his glove at Alfredo's feet. With a swooping motion, Alfredo picks up the challenge and stiffly leaves the room. And as his father walks sadly after him, the orchestra repeats six rapid chords followed by four slow ones that bring the act to a close.

ACT III

Although Verdi wanted the short piece of music that comes before the act (the prelude) to be played while we are looking at the opening scene, sometimes the curtain does not go up until the music ends. And sometimes we do see the scene through a veil-like curtain called a scrim.

We hear the sad melody telling us of Violetta's serious illness. We hear the violins sobbing, sobbing...as (quivering) they softly come to an end.

In a shabby bedroom Violetta is lying there in the gloom. As we once again hear the music of the prelude, she awakens and calls for Annina.

"Were you asleep, poor girl?"

"Yes, forgive me...."

"Let me have a little water. See if it is daytime...."

Annina gently helps the sick girl take a sip of water. She tells her that it is seven in the morning. Violetta wants a little light so Annina opens the curtains and shutters. From there she sees Doctor Grenville coming up to the front door. Violetta is happy to hear this and wants to get up to greet "her true friend." As she tries to rise—helped by Annina—we hear the sobbing violins again.

It is only with the doctor's help that Violetta can make her painful way to the sofa.

"...How are you feeling...?"

"My body is suffering...but my soul is at peace..."

She tells the doctor that she did have a restful sleep. But when the doctor assures her that she will soon get well, Violetta isn't fooled.

"Goodbye," says the doctor, pressing her hand, "I'll see you later."

The worried Annina follows Doctor Grenville to the door and softly asks him about her mistress. And he, under his breath, mournfully tells her that Violetta really has only a few hours more to live.

However, Violetta feels a bit more comfortable and asks Annina if it is a holiday. Yes! It is Carnival time and all of Paris has gone crazy! It may be a holiday for some, yet Violetta wonders about all the people who are suffering—even though it seems the whole city is celebrating.

"How much money do we have left...?"

"Twenty louis."

"Give ten to the poor...."

"But you'll have only a little left!"

"Oh...there'll be enough for me...then, get me the mail...."

When Annina leaves, we hear the violins once more—but they now sound feverish. As Violetta takes out a worn letter from her night gown, the violins lead into the beautiful love theme we heard in the first act. In a sorrowful speaking voice Violetta reads once again the old letter (which she really knows by heart). It is from Alfredo's father.

> "You have kept your promise...the Baron was wounded, but will be all right...Alfredo left...I myself, told him of your sacrifice...and he is returning to ask you to forgive him. I will come to see you too. Get well. You deserve a better future...."

Halfway through the letter we see that Violetta knows it so well that she is no longer looking at it! When she ends...she painfully gets up and looks in her mirror. Seeing how pale and wasted she is she cries two of the most pitiful words in opera— "It's late!"

She has waited and waited. Will they ever come? The doctor has tried to give her hope...but with this disease she knows that all hope is dead. Her voice rises and lingers on the word "dead." Then to a longing and sad melody she sings her good-bye to all her happy dreams of the past! As she sings we hear the word "traviata." She, "the lost one," asks God to forgive her. And with a final high note she realizes that at last..."all, all...is ended!"

The aria (with the oboe playing the melody) is barely finished when, from outside, we hear a bunch of merrymakers celebrating Carnival time! They all end in a burst of laughter. It is so different from Violetta's song that we pity her all the more.

Then the orchestra begins. Annina hurries in. The music is getting louder.

"My lady..."

"What's the matter?"

"Will you promise to stay calm?"

"Yes...what are you telling me...?"

"...an unexpected surprise..."

We hear the music building, building...until in a dramatic musical climax Alfredo enters and folds Violetta into his arms as their voices soar together in happiness!

To excited, quick music the lovers are together again at last!

"Forgive me...and my father...!"

They shall be together forever! The music rises, rises to a wonderful crashing ending as the two young lovers repeat, "No, no, no...nothing can part us now!"

Alfredo slowly helps Violetta to the sofa and, still holding her in his arms, he sings a melodious aria telling her that they will now leave Paris and live happily ever after! Violetta wants this to be true. Soon she repeats this wish with the same lilting melody and finally, together, they sing about their future life and to the day when Violetta's health will "bloom again." The duet flows to a sweet end.

But as Violetta had said, it is too late. She sways. Alfredo sees that she has become very pale! The music shows his alarm. And Violetta, not able to sit up anymore, slowly rests herself on the couch.

"Good God! Violetta!"

"...It was nothing. Annina, help me get dressed...."

"Now?" asks Alfredo. "Let's wait..."

"No...I want to go out!"

But when Annina tries to help her, Violetta is much too weak. She falls back again.

"Good God...I can't!"

"Call the doctor!"

"Tell him," cries Violetta to Annina, "that Alfredo is back with me...that I want to live...!"

The music strikes a desperate note.

And then, turning to Alfredo, she tells him that if *his* returning to her cannot save her...then nothing on earth can ever do so! The orchestra bursts into sound.

With her last bit of strength she pushes herself up from the sofa and with a desperate cry to God she asks why should she die...so young...now when at last "she can dry her tears...?" Alfredo sings with her asking her not to give up all hope. And as their voices climb, Violetta is heard singing...

"Oh, Alfredo...what a cruel ending...to our love...!"

Now Giorgio Germont comes forth to greet her.

"I'm keeping my promise...and you are as my own daughter to me...."

But Violetta, without bitterness, tells him he has come too late! She is at least dying in the arms of those she loves most in the world! The old man quickly sees that she is really deathly ill.

"Ah, foolish old man...I can now see all the harm that I did!"

Violetta asks Alfredo to come closer to her. The orchestra sounds steady low notes as she tells her loved one that she will give him a little framed picture of herself so that he will not forget her. All five voices join in. Alfredo pleads that she must not die! His father again asks her for forgiveness. Annina will always remember her and cry at the memory.

Then in a small voice, Violetta asks Alfredo to give her portrait to the young girl whom he will some day meet and marry. "Tell her," says Violetta, "that it is a gift from someone who is praying in heaven for her and for you...."

As the blend of voices comes to a close we again hear the violins playing the early love theme.

Suddenly, Violetta feels new strength in her body! All her pains are gone! She's coming "back to life!" While joyfully crying out about her strange new feeling (the violins set up a shaking sound),

Violetta falls lifeless into Alfredo's arms! And with the orchestra pounding out the closing strains of the opera—Alfredo calls to Violetta while the others mourn this tragic end.

THE CURTAIN FALLS

And so the young girl—so beautiful, so fragile, so full of life that she easily captured the Paris world of the 1840's—died at the age of twenty-three. Her story has been played by the great Sarah Bernhardt right up to the great Greta Garbo in the movie entitled *Camille*.

The first performance of the opera took place in Venice at La Fenice (Lah Fen-EECH-eh)—The Phoenix Opera House—on March 6, 1853. According to Verdi it was not a success—to *him*. To the audience it was wonderful. Verdi was known to be a pessimist, so when he heard the tenor sounding a bit hoarse, and saw the soprano (who was supposed to be wasted away from tuberculosis) looking a bit fat, he thought the whole thing was a fiasco. The real truth was described by Tommaso Locatelli, a well-known critic at that time: "The public was ravished by the most beautiful and lively melodies that have been heard in a long time..."

La Traviata was repeated ten times in that first season alone! It easily joined *Il Trovatore* and *Rigoletto* to become the third star of Verdi's "middle period." And so Verdi, along with his librettist Francesco Maria Piave, had another hit on his hands—one that has never left the great opera stages of the world.

It was introduced in America on December 3, 1856 at the New York Academy of Music. And when the old Metropolitan was built in 1883, *La Traviata* was presented in the very first season on November 5, less than a month after the house opened.

As we have said before, Verdi was never again to write an opera that was so "intimate"...about real people of his own time.

But, standing in the wings, there was soon to appear another composer who was to become the most brilliant of writers about "real people."

(This opens up the question as to whether this composer is a *verismo* —down to earth, true to life—composer or not. Some say his music is too romantic, the words he uses too poetic, to put him in the *verismo* camp. Others argue, what could be any more *verismo* than the story about a bunch of struggling young Bohemians? Or the one about a girl who has a baby and is forced to become a nun—*Suor Angelica:* Sister Angelica? Or the story about a rough, pipe-smoking boat captain who murders one of his workers for trying to take away his young wife...then covers him up with his overcoat—*Il Tabarro:* The Overcoat? It seems fair to say that this composer was a master of both worlds, a genius who could take the best of those worlds and blend them into a single beautiful masterpiece.)

His name is Giacomo Puccini (JAH-ko-mo Poo-CHEE-nee), a boy who "inherited" music beginning with his great-great-grandfather for whom he was named. It was with this ancestor that the family started to become organists and choirmasters at the Cathedral of San Martino in the very old walled city of Lucca.

As the boy grew up, it did not seem as if he would be very good at doing anything musical. But his uncle kept him at the organ and kept kicking him in the shins every time he hit a sour note. He was lucky, however, to get another teacher, Carlo Angeloni, who not only made him a better organ player but also opened up his ears to the music of Giuseppe Verdi! So little by little—even though he would rather listen to the river and the birds (mixed in with having a few girlfriends)—Puccini learned music and how to compose. Finally, he took the step that would lead him to becoming one of the world's best-loved composers.

Not far from Lucca is the town of Pisa with its famous leaning tower. It also had the opera house called the Teatro Verdi. And Puccini, now just about eighteen, packed up something to eat, took along two of his best friends and walked the over twenty miles to the opera house to see the wonderful new Verdi opera *Aida!* Well, by the time he got back home (early the next morning) he was filled with the music he had heard. Soon he began composing and becoming known. But how was he, a very poor boy, to continue his studies in the important city of Milan?

It took his mother, whom he adored, to speak to a lady she knew slightly who was part of the Queen's court. After waiting anxiously for word from Queen Margherita, Puccini was at last awarded a scholarship to the conservatory! He was now just twenty-two years old.

The years that followed certainly prepared him for writing his most loved opera—*La Boheme*. This is the work we will soon enjoy. But first let's stay with the young man who struggled to keep warm, to find something to eat...and who had to sell his overcoat for a few *lire* so that he could dine and dance with a girl from the La Scala opera chorus! He truly lived the life of a *Bohemian!* So, when he read Henry Murger's story called *Scenes from the Bohemian Life (Scenes de la vie de Boheme)* it surely hit home.

By this time, however, Puccini had had his first big success with an opera about a young girl (very much like Violetta) whose name was *Manon Lescaut*. Money began pouring in; and so we find him in his thirties living in the Villa Puccini in a little town called Tower of the Lake...or, in Italian, Torre del Lago. (The lake itself is called the tongue-twisting Massaciuccoli. Today the town is officially named Torre del Lago Puccini.) He is married to Elvira and has a nine year old son, Antonio.

And he is working hard on his Bohemian Girl—*La Boheme*. At last on February 1, 1896, in the Teatro Regio (in the city of Turin, Italy) the premiere of this beloved opera takes place.

It brings us once again to Paris, the Paris of 1838. But this time we are on the other side of the river Seine—the left bank—and not in the rich homes of the demi-mond. Here are the poor artists and poets...and girls...trying to stay alive and to get a bit of joy out of the bohemian life they lead. It is the Latin Quarter...Montmartre...the place where we meet the pretty eighteen year old girl known as...

7

La Boheme

(Lah Boe-EM)

Before we hear the three deep opening notes of the opera, let me mention one of the most important things about this wonderful work. It is an opera that is—and will be—forever young. For there will always be young people struggling to make a living, always falling in love, and out of love—always dreaming, hoping, looking for peace and happiness. And whether a person is just starting out in life, or has lived awhile, there will always be the remembering of dreams, of love, and of hopes that never die. And now let's join some young people that Puccini knew so well from his own early days when he, too, was poor and struggling.

ACT I

The scene is a scruffy garret—a room at the top of a building—that looks out over the roofs of Paris. A bit of smoke from the chimneys is seen. It is a cold, snowy, Christmas Eve. There is Marcello (Mahr-CHELL-o) in a corner painting *The Red Sea* of the Bible. He tells Rodolfo (Roe-DAHL-foe), the poet, that looking at the water is making him feel numb..."as if it was raining on him!" And to make himself feel better he's going to "drown" the pharaoh!

Rodolfo has been looking out the large garret window watching the lazy smoke. He complains that the little iron stove is as lazy as a rich lord. They have no fuel for it and they're both freezing to death, as well as dying from hunger.

They must have a fire. Marcello has an idea. How about burning the chair? But Rodolfo stops him because he has a better idea. Eureka! Marcello thinks he wants to burn his painting, but Rodolfo tells him that it would smell too much.

"My drama...its passion will warm us! Here's the first act!"

Marcello quickly takes the paper, tears it a little and starts a fire. It's a cheerful blaze and they try to make the most of it. As they're busy warming their hands, in comes Colline (Ko-LEEN) who has been trying to sell some of his books.

Colline is a long-haired philosopher. He complains that even on Christmas Eve he can't get anyone to offer him a little money for his books. Then he spots the fire. He's amazed at this unexpected warmth!

"Quiet," says Rodolfo, "they're giving my play..."

"...to the fire!" comments Colline. "I find it brilliant!"

"And lively," says Rodolfo.

"But it doesn't last long," Colline remarks, sadly, as the music tells us the fire is dying out.

So page after page is burned away while the three make sarcastic fun of the play.

"That was a deep thought!"

"Perfect color"

"...A love scene goes up in smoke!"

"A page crackles."

"That's where the kisses are!"

Finally, Rodolfo decides he wants to "hear" all three acts at once so he throws the whole thing into the fire. But before long they see the flames once again getting smaller and smaller and the fire slowly dies out. At this, both Marcello and Colline point an accusing finger at Rodolfo.

"Down with the author!"

Suddenly two boys come in carrying wood, cigars, wine and food! The three men are amazed. Schaunard (Show-NARD) the musician proudly walks in and throws some coins on the floor! Now they're really amazed. Marcello can't believe his eyes so he calls the coins a fake—"pieces of tin!" Schaunard is insulted.

"Are you deaf...blind?"

He takes a coin and asks them to tell him who is pictured on it.

"Louis-Phillip!"

They are really French coins and soon Schaunard begins telling them that he earned all this money by giving music lessons to an Englishman. Meanwhile, Marcello starts to set the table. Rodolfo starts another fire, this time with real wood! They're doing anything but listening to Schaunard. Finally, he tells them all to go to the devil. He also notices that they're about to eat the food he brought so he takes everything and puts it away. He wants to save it all for "the dark and gloomy future." He also thinks that it's foolish to stay home on Christmas Eve when outside is the delicious smell of cooking sausages...plus the smiles of young girls.

"Let's drink at home...but let's eat out!"

He no sooner gets the words out when there's a knock on the door. A shaky, old voice asks,

"May I come in?"

"Who is it?"

"Benoit (Ben-WAH)!"

The orchestra crashes. It's the landlord!

Schaunard wants to shut the door in his face. Colline calls out that there's no one at home. Schaunard tells him, "We're closed!" But Benoit, from the other side of the door, pleads for just one word. So Schaunard lets him in but tells him that he can only say one, single word. This doesn't really bother Benoit because his one word is, "Rent!"

They all leap into action. One gives Benoit a chair. Another gets out the wine. Glasses are filled. A toast! So while they're busy getting Benoit drunk, he's trying to collect the rent.

"It's the last quarter of the year...," he says.

"That's nice," says Marcello.

Meanwhile, his glass is filled again. He's beginning to get tipsy, but still talks about their promise to pay him. Marcello points to the coins on the table. The others think he's crazy. But Marcello knows what he's doing. He's going to get Benoit drunk enough so that he'll forget the rent.

"...stay awhile. How old are you?"

"More or less our own age," teases Rodolfo.

"More...much more," says Benoit, seriously.

"Well, we did say more or less," adds Colline.

Marcello now brings up the fact that Benoit was caught flirting with a pretty girl the other night. What? You rascal!

"I'm old, yes...but strong...."

Benoit goes on to tell them that although he was very shy as a boy, he's now making up for it. As he tells them about the kind of girls he likes—pleasantly plump—he mentions his wife. Well, that's all the boys have to hear! You have a wife? You bad man! Get out! Get out! And before Benoit knows what's happened he finds himself out in the hall and the door locked!

With Benoit gone they get down to business. They share the money. Marcello hands Colline a mirror and tells him that he should, at last, stop looking like a bear and get his hair cut. Colline agrees.

"For the first time, I'll get to know a barber!"

All right, let's go. Rodolfo now tells them that he's got a few more lines to write for a magazine, but will be with them in five minutes. They'll wait for him downstairs, but don't be long.

As they leave, Marcello calls out that they had better hold on to the railing or they'll fall down the dark stairs. Rodolfo hears a crash and Colline's voice.

"Colline, are you dead?"

"Not yet!"

"Come on, hurry!" calls Marcello.

The voices fade. Rodolfo sits down and tries to write. He tears up the paper and throws his pen down. He doesn't seem to be in the mood. Then there's a soft knock at the door.

With this small sound and Rodolfo's question, "Who is there?" Puccini begins one of the most touching, beautiful, intimate scenes in opera. It is the meeting of two young people for the first time. Both are lonely and have little more than their youth. Life, so far, has been cruel, but they have tried to make the best of it. What will their future be and will they face it together?

"Excuse me," cries a girl's voice.

It's a woman! Rodolfo smooths his hair a bit. The voice tells him that the candle has gone out. As Rodolfo opens the door we hear the love-theme music that will be repeated as the opera unfolds.

"Please come in...."

Mimi (Mee-mee) hesitates. She timidly walks a few steps but is suddenly faint. Rodolfo is worried, but Mimi tells him that she is just out of breath from climbing the stairs. But as she sits in the chair she passes out!

The candle and her key drop from her hands. "Well...*now* what do I do?" Rodolfo wonders aloud. Finally he decides to sprinkle a few drops of water on her face...while the violins plink along with him.

He sees that the young girl really looks very sick. As he bends over her, she comes to and Rodolfo asks her if she is feeling better.

"Yes..."

"Come sit by the fire...it's so cold in here...."

Rodolfo doesn't know what else to do to make her more comfortable—and to get better acquainted! He offers her some wine. As she drinks a little, he thinks of how lovely she is.

But Mimi takes up her candle and starts to leave. Rodolfo tries to convince her to stay awhile...but she bids him goodnight and goes. A second later she's back. She can't find her key! And to make things worse, the drafty hallway has put out her candle again.

This gives Rodolfo an idea. He secretly blows out his own candle! Now begins a little duel—Mimi trying to find her key so she can go to her room, while Rodolfo not only isn't looking too hard for the key, but also when he does find it he hides it!

"Have you found it?"

"No," fibs Rodolfo.

"I thought..."

"No, truly..."

"Are you still looking?"

"I'm looking!"

And then, as they are on their hands and knees groping in the dark, their hands touch. Mimi gives a small cry.

With the touch of these hands, Puccini now gives us two of the most beautiful, most moving arias ever composed.

"What a frozen little hand...," sings Rodolfo. "Let me warm it for you..."

He goes on to tell her that the chances of finding her key in the dark are not too good. But there's a lovely moon...

Mimi tries to draw her hand away.

"Wait...young lady...in two words I'll tell you who I am, what I do, and how I live..."

Rodolfo is a poet...a poor, but light-hearted one. He has the soul of a millionaire...for he can easily dream and have visions of castles in the air. But once in a while these jewel-like thoughts are taken from him by two "thieves"—the beautiful eyes of a beautiful girl! In fact, "they came in with you" and sure enough they stole all other thoughts from his head. However, he's looking forward hopefully...!

"Well," says Rodolfo, "now that you know *me*...would you mind telling me about yourself? Please..."

"Yes," murmurs Mimi. "They call me Mimi, but my name is Lucia."

She hasn't much of a story to tell him. She embroiders linen or silk, in her room or outside. She's happy and she just loves to make roses and lilies. She, too, loves dreams and visions...springtime...all the things that are poetic. She stops a moment to ask Rodolfo if he understands. Of course he does!

So Mimi goes on. In a little-girl voice she says she doesn't really know why they call her Mimi. She eats by herself, doesn't always go to church, but she prays a lot to the Lord. Alone in her small white room she sees the roofs and sky...and when spring comes (here the music opens and swells) "...the first sunshine is mine...the first kiss of April is mine!" A rose in her vase is blossoming—and she watches it bloom leaf after leaf—but, unfortunately the flowers that *she* makes have no odor. . . .

That's all there is to tell. . .except that, "I'm your neighbor who is bothering you. . . ." The young girl looks up at him from her chair.

Before Rodolfo has time to answer, his friends call from below. They've been waiting awhile and are dying to get to the Cafe Momus (Moe-moose).

"Hey, Rodolfo!"

Rodolfo explains to Mimi that these are his friends.

"What are you doing up there by yourself?"

"I'm not alone," calls Rodolfo from the window. "Go along to Momus and save a place for two. . . ."

And so the three go on their way singing about getting to the cafe. Once again Rodolfo turns to Mimi. Things have been happening between them. . .in their eyes, in their thoughts. Rodolfo goes to her and begins a sweet love song.

"Oh lovely girl. . .in you I see dreams that I would like to dream forever!"

Mimi, too, finds love awakening in her. Two young people, alone. . .leading struggling lives. . .trying to find happiness. Rodolfo tries to kiss her. She draws away.

"Your friends are waiting for you."

"Are you sending me away so soon?"

Then Mimi starts to ask him something, but hesitates. He urges her to speak. Finally, she says she would like to go with him. But Rodolfo has other ideas! He tells her that it would be so nice to stay right where they are—it's so *cold* outside. Mimi coyly tells him that she will be near him to keep warm.

"And when we get back?" asks Rodolfo.

"Funny man!" whispers Mimi, with a little laugh.

Now Rodolfo holds out his arm to her with great style. The music opens up. He asks her to give him her arm. Mimi, playing along with the game, tells him that she will obey him. . ."my lord". . .And as the two young people leave arm in arm we can hear Rodolfo beg Mimi to tell him she loves him. "I love you," she declares as her voice rises. And then, as they slowly walk out of sight down the hall, we hear them both declare their love— their voices reaching ever higher and higher— "Love. . .love. . .love. . ."

The curtain falls on the little garret in Paris on the eve of Christmas.

ACT II

It is the Latin Quarter outside the Cafe Momus! There are crowds of people—small boys and girls running about, street vendors shouting their wares, students, working-girls, mothers pulling at their children! It is so crowded that tables have been set up outside the cafe.

"Oranges, dates! Hot chestnuts!"

"What a crowd!"

Everyone is bustling around. . .shoving, pushing, buying. . . customers calling to waiters, Schaunard trying out a horn, Colline looking at the coat he has just bought.

"It's just a little bit used. . . ."

"Let's go," Rodolfo tells Mimi. "Hold tight to my arm."

Marcello, who had a fight with his steady girl, Musetta, is bitter.

"I'd like to shout. . .which of you girls would care for a bit of love!"

He keeps flirting, but his heart really isn't in it. Colline has just found a rare copy of a book on grammar.

"Let's eat," grumbles Marcello.

Schaunard and Colline want to know where Rodolfo went.

"Into a milliner's shop."

Just then Rodolfo appears with Mimi. He has just bought her a pink bonnet.

"Is the color all right for me?"

"You're a brunette so the color is just right...."

And so it goes. Everyone crowding about. Rodolfo promising to buy Mimi a fine necklace—better than the one in the window—as soon as his rich uncle passes on!

Finally, the two lovers arrive at the cafe. Rodolfo's friends, of course, are already there. He introduces them to Mimi.

"...Her arrival completes this lovely gathering...this fine company...From my head springs poetry...from her fingers, flowers—and from both our happy souls: Love!"

At this, the three friends burst out laughing, but they all accept Mimi at once.

In the distance, we hear the sound of a familiar toy-seller named Parpignol (Par-peen-YOL). His cart is gaily decorated...and he is soon surrounded by boys and girls, all begging for this toy or that one. While mothers are trying to tear them away, we hear the children shout for a trumpet, the little horse, the cannon...

Schaunard orders roasted venison from the waiter. Marcello wants a turkey! Rhine wine! Table wine! Lobster!

They're surely living high—especially since they have very little money!

Marcello asks Mimi what great gift Rodolfo has bought her. She shows him her bonnet which "goes with my dark hair. "Rodolfo," she tells Marcello, "knows what is in my heart...and he is very smart.''

"So much so that what he says actually seems true,'' teases Schaunard.

When Mimi comments that love is sweeter than honey, Marcello bitterly says that love can be honey or poison!

It seems that Marcello's fickle girl-friend left him for a better life...for someone with money. And just as he is about to "drown his sorrow" in a glass of wine...in walks Musetta with her old money-bags.

Now follows a comical scene in which Musetta tries to get Marcello back again, while he tries to ignore her. Here she sings a catchy, tempting song known as "Musetta's Waltz.''

"...When I walk alone...everyone stops to stare...trying to see all my beauty—from top to toe...''

At this Marcello growls, "Tie me to the chair!''

Of course, the unlucky old gentleman that she came with is greatly embarrassed and tries to keep her quiet and not make a scene. All along Musetta is trying to see if she's getting anywhere with Marcello. His friends are sure that he will give in and they will get together again. Finally, when Musetta sees that she really has Marcello's attention, she pulls a trick on her rich escort. Suddenly she screams!

"What's the matter?'' cries old Alcindoro (Ahl-cheen-DORO).

"What pain! What burning!''

"Where?''

"In my foot!''

Quickly Musetta tells Alcindoro to take off her pinching shoe and take it to be fixed. Marcello is now beaming. And as the poor old man hurries off, Marcello and Musetta fall into each other's arms! At the same time the waiter brings the bill!

"So soon?'' asks Schaunard.

"Who asked for it?" complains Colline.

Naturally they soon find that they have about thirty cents among them—they're broke!

Meanwhile, in the distance, we hear the drums of a soldier's marching band. Musetta grabs the waiter and tells him to put the boys' bill with hers and that her old "friend" will pay both checks as soon as he gets back!

And so while the sound of the drums gets closer—the children beg their mothers to let them see—the four young men, along with Musetta and Mimi, get ready to follow the band. The drum major now marches in followed by the others. And as they pass by, everybody starts marching behind—Musetta is carried by Marcello and Colline, while Rodolfo and Mimi are arm in arm.

Suddenly old Alcindoro hurries in only to find his companion gone and the waiter presenting him with two bills. He falls back into a chair—stupified—as the curtain falls. This whole lively scene is full of Puccini melodies—blending and weaving in and out—with glorious voices to match.

ACT III

This little act is like a small jewel set against the snow. Almost two months have passed since that happy Christmas Eve. It is now early one morning in February. The ground is covered with new-fallen snow...some puffy flakes are still coming down.

There are the Gates of Iron...one of Paris' toll-gates. Some workers and peasant girls are coming into the city. The girls talk about meeting later at noon. A sergeant questions a passer-by with a basket, looks inside, then passes on.

Meanwhile we have seen Mimi. We also hear her melody from the first act. She has asked the sergeant to point out the tavern where a painter is working. It's right there. She then asks a maid who has come out of the tavern if she would kindly ask Marcello to come out to meet her.

"Tell him, softly, that Mimi is waiting for him...."

Marcello appears hurriedly, surprised to see Mimi. He and Musetta have been at the tavern for about a month—she gives singing lessons while he paints some soldiers on the front of the building. We hear the strains of Musetta's waltz. Mimi is sick. She begins to cough. Marcello is worried about her and asks her to come inside to get warm. But she can't. Rodolfo is inside, asleep. She pleads for help from Marcello. Rodolfo is full of jealousy—suspicious of everything she does. He keeps telling her to find herself another man—"You're not for me...."

Marcello tries to show her that they are too serious together, she and Rodolfo.

"You are right...we must part...."

Mimi coughs once more. She's had a chill since the day before and Rodolfo left her last night telling her that it was all over between them. She is desperate. (Now the two sing a thrilling duet that goes straight to your heart.) Then, looking through the window, Marcello notices that Rodolfo is waking up and about to search for him. He warns Mimi to leave, but she hides a short distance away. We hear the love theme.

"Marcello. At last! No one can hear us here. I want to be separated from Mimi!"

Marcello calls him a fool for taking love so seriously...he should have more laughter...for without fun, love is weak and ugly. Then he starts to tell his friend all the things that are wrong with him.

"You're   jealous...crazy...prejudiced...annoying...stubborn!"

Mimi worries that this will only make Rodolfo more angry with her. Then in a sweeping melody Rodolfo tries to convince Marcello that Mimi is just a flirt and no good. But Marcello doesn't believe him. And so Rodolfo finally tells him the truth. His voice soars as he admits that he loves Mimi more than anything else in the world, but that he is tortured by the fear that she is getting sicker and sicker...

"The poor little thing is doomed...!"

(Mimi is surprised to hear this and in a small wondering voice asks, "Oh my, am I dying?")

In a haunting melody Rodolfo continues: Mimi has a terrible cough...she is pale, yet flushed. His room is a sloppy den...cold and damp...and although Mimi sings and smiles—he is the cause of the sickness that is killing her!

We hear Mimi's voice from her hiding place. Then all three voices blend. Suddenly Rodolfo hears her crying and coughing. He hurries to her and tries to get her out of the cold. (Has she heard what he has said?) Mimi can't go inside because the smoke will make her worse.

Then Musetta's laughter is heard. Marcello wonders if she is flirting with someone. He rushes to see.

Rodolfo and Mimi are now alone. The snow falls lazily as the music introduces one of the most beautiful—yet sad—duets in opera. Mimi mournfully tells him that she will return once more to the little room that she had left to answer his call of love.

"Goodbye," she sings, "but without hard feelings...I'll go back to making flowers. Listen...listen...put together the few things I leave behind. In my little case there is locked that little gold ring and my prayer book. Make up a bundle and I'll send the porter to pick it up. Oh...and look under my pillow. You'll find the pink bonnet. If you want to...keep it as a memory of our love...! (Her voice cries out.) Goodbye...goodbye...but without hard feelings...!"

Rodolfo realizes that this then is truly the end.

"You are going away, my little one...Goodbye to dreams of love..."

In contrast, Mimi answers, "Goodbye to quarrels and jealousy..."

"...that you would quiet with a smile...," reminds

Rodolfo.

"Goodbye to suspicions...," sings Mimi.

"...to kisses...," sings Rodolfo.

But then together they realize...that to be alone in winter-time..."one could die of loneliness...." (Their voices float up with great love.)

"Alone...," whispers Mimi, dreading the thought.

"While in the spring we have the company of the sun," Rodolfo mentions hopefully.

The two parting lovers are interrupted from their dreaming by an argument between Marcello and Musetta. They come out of the tavern with Marcello accusing Musetta of flirting with that man near the fireplace. With this, the duet becomes a quartet. All four voices rise ever higher. Rodolfo and Mimi still wondering if they should part, while Marcello and Musetta are storming at each other.

"No one is alone in April," we hear Mimi say.

"...and the roses...," says Rodolfo.

"From every nest there is a gentle chirping," recalls Mimi.

But the other two are fighting.

"Why are you shouting at me? Why this song and dance? We weren't united at the altar!" Musetta shouts.

And so while Rodolfo and Mimi are slowly beginning to think that perhaps they should stay together until "the season of the flowers," Musetta and Marcello are telling each other to get lost!

"Tavern painter!"

"Viper!"

"Toad!"

"Witch!"

The fighters are now gone.

"I'll always be yours...for life," swears Mimi. (Even

though they shall part..."when the flowers bloom again...")

"I wish the winter would last an eternity!" sings Mimi, as they slowly walk off, together once again. Their voices soar and then grow faint, declaring once more that they will part when the season of the flowers arrives. They will stay together until springtime! The curtain slowly falls.

ACT IV

When the curtain rises we find ourselves back in the same miserable garret room where the story started. The orchestra opens with powerful chords. Then we hear the same notes that began the opera. Rodolfo is at his table trying to write, while Marcello is not getting very far trying to paint. Once again, Puccini's genius creates a gorgeous picture in melody. The violins sweetly speak of the lost loves—the memory of Mimi and Musetta—as the two men try not to seem too eager.

Rodolfo mentions that he saw Musetta dressed all in velvet in a rich carriage pulled by a pair of fine horses.

"I'm happy to hear that," lies Marcello. "I also saw..."

"Musetta?" asks Rodolfo.

"Mimi. She was in a carriage dressed like a queen."

"Great! I'm glad to hear it..."

We hear Marcello mumbling to himself, "The liar—he's dying of love." So they both try to get back to work. But it's no use.

"What a terrible pen!"

"What a terrible brush!"

Rodolfo dreams of Mimi, while Marcello thinks of Musetta. The duet, in a sorrowful melody, tells of how much they love the girls and how much they miss them. Rodolfo still has the little pink bonnet that Mimi left him.

Then just as Rodolfo wonders about Schaunard, in he comes

carrying some loaves of bread. Colline's contribution is a single herring! Now the mood changes. All four make believe that they're having a big feast.

"Let's put the champagne on ice," says Schaunard, as he stands a bottle of water in Colline's hat.

And so they go on pretending that they're eating "parrot's tongue" and other good things, as they call each other "duke" and "baron." Colline gets up to say that he has a date to see the king. Schaunard announces that he just feels like singing...but the other three shout, "No!" Well, how about some dancing? To this they agree and they begin to move the chairs and table to one side.

The violins start a minuet. Heels click as Schaunard switches to a fandango. Colline suggests a quadrille—so all four start to dance. One or two become "girls" with high voices to match. In a moment, Colline starts an argument about the kind of dancing that should come first. This leads to a "duel" between him and Schaunard—one with the stove tongs, the other with the shovel. Meanwhile, Rodolfo and Marcello are dancing all around them.

Suddenly we hear the violins scream. Musetta rushes in to tell them that Mimi is on the stairs exhausted! Rodolfo rushes out to help her while the others prepare the bed.

"Oh my Rodolfo...do you want me here with you?"

"Always, always...my Mimi..."

Musetta had heard that Mimi had left her rich friend and that she was dying. She searched and searched and finally saw Mimi on a street, hardly able to walk. When Musetta went to her, Mimi told her that she could no longer go on—and that all she wanted was to die close to Rodolfo.

Now Mimi is looking around telling her friends how happy she is to be with them. Then (as with Verdi's Violetta), she suddenly feels stronger. Her voice flies up gracefully. Musetta asks Marcello if there is any coffee or wine. He sadly answers that there is nothing here but poverty. Privately Schaunard tells Colline that "she'll be dead in a half-hour."

"I'm so cold," says Mimi. "If I only had a muff. Will I ever be able to warm these hands of mine?"

Then she looks at them all and greets them in a small, frail voice.

"Good day...Marcello, Schaunard, Colline...good day. All of you are here...smiling at Mimi..."

Then as Rodolfo begs her to stay quiet, Mimi tells Marcello that Musetta is really a good girl.

"I know, I know...."

Musetta takes off her earrings. She wants Marcello to sell them, buy some liqueur (actually a pain-killer called laudanum) and call a doctor. Then she has another idea. She tells Marcello that asking for a little muff may really be Mimi's dying wish so she's going to get one for her. They both leave.

To one side we see Colline. He owns nothing but his great-coat. Slowly he takes it off. In a little aria (that can stop the show if done to perfection) he bids farewell to his "dear old coat." As he rolls it up he sings his thanks to this faithful friend whose pockets had sheltered the books written by philosophers and poets.

"Now that happy days are gone...I bid you farewell, my faithful friend, farewell...."

Turning to Schaunard he suggests that they leave the lovers to themselves...and with a sad look at their dear friends they slowly go out the door. A short bit of music recalls when Rodolfo first introduced himself to Mimi. Mimi opens her eyes and tells him shyly that she pretended to be asleep so that they might be alone together. And then she sings some of the most touching words in opera...

"There are so many things I want to tell you..."

Her voice rises as she sings that he is her love, her life.

"Ah, Mimi...my beautiful Mimi!"

"Am I still beautiful?"

"As beautiful as the dawn...."

But Mimi says that he must mean "beautiful as the sunset" (as she feels herself dying). In a dreamy voice she remembers their first meeting.

"They call me Mimi...but why...I don't know...."

Rodolfo tries to comfort her. Now she has returned home to her "nest" like the swallow. Then he surprises her with the little pink bonnet! Excited to see it, Mimi recalls when she first came through his door. They both remember their words spoken so long ago.

"What a frozen little hand," sings Mimi, reminding him of his touch.

But a fit of coughing ends her song. Rodolfo is alarmed. Schaunard returns followed by Musetta and Marcello.

"...the doctor is coming; I told him to hurry. Here's the cordial."

Musetta gives Mimi the muff she has just bought. She is thrilled at the thought that her hands will now at last be warm!

"Is it from you?" she asks Rodolfo.

But before he can answer, Musetta quickly tells her that it is.

Rodolfo can no longer keep from crying. Mimi tries to help by telling him that she will always be with him. Her voice weakens as she says that her hands are now warm at last. She becomes unconscious!

On the little side table Musetta has lit a small burner to warm the liqueur. She prays to the Blessed Virgin not to let Mimi die.

"Holy Virgin...I'm not worthy to be pardoned...but Mimi is an angel from heaven...."

But it is too late. Schaunard whispers to Marcello that the girl has died!

Rodolfo, meanwhile, has been at the window trying to shade the light. He turns. Colline asks him how Mimi is doing. Rodolfo remarks that he can see that she's peaceful. Suddenly he notices Marcello and Schaunard looking at each other. He begins to fear the worst!

"Why are you looking at me like that!" cries Rodolfo.

And as Marcello asks him to have courage, Rodolfo now knows that Mimi is really gone! He twice cries out her name...sobbing...while the orchestra's horns, cymbals, violins and drums bring all their power to the sorrowful scene. Then the music gradually dies away.

THE CURTAIN FALLS

...on the lives of friends whom we have met at the height of their youth. And although "youth lasts for but a day," as Juliette tells us, this little band of Bohemians will never grow old; their youth will always be with us through the immortal music of Giacomo Puccini. Was there really a Mimi? Yes. At the age of 24, Lucile Louvet died on April 9, 1848 of tuberculosis, in bed no. 8 in the Hopital de la Pitie (Hospital for the Poor), Paris.

It's been almost one hundred years since the twenty-seven year old Arturo Toscanini (the most famous conductor of our time) led the opening notes of *La Boheme*. Strangely enough, the critics were not too kind! But what the critics didn't like the audience did—*Boheme* was performed no fewer than twenty-four times during that month of February.

But it was not until it reached Palermo, Sicily, in the Politeama Garibaldi Theatre in April, Friday the 13th, that *Boheme* took off. The audience went wild; Puccini was called on stage and remained there to frantic applause. The last act had to be repeated, even though Mimi was now in street clothes and the tenor had no makeup!

It had taken Puccini about four years to compose *Boheme*, all the while driving his librettists, Giuseppe Giacosa and Luigi Illica, almost crazy with details. Giulio Ricordi (Puccini's publisher) had all he could do to keep them both from resigning! But the result of all the arguments and angry letters is a work so perfectly put together that it is impossible to take even one line out of it.

It is not surprising then to find the English critic, Frank Granville Barker (writing about the Mimi of Victoria De los Angeles and the Rodolfo of Jussi Bjoerling, two great stars) saying: "The man or woman who is insensitive to the spell of this performance really isn't fit to live in civilized society—for it is one of the wonders of the world."

The spell of *La Boheme* began in the United States on October 14, 1897 in the Los Angeles Theatre when it was performed by the little Del Conte Italian Opera Company of Milan. And three years later, December 26, 1900, it arrived at the Metropolitan Opera House, starring the fabulous Nellie Melba and the unforgettable Enrico Caruso.

Although Puccini's next opera was the very successful and very dramatic story about an actress named Floria Tosca, let's first meet a little girl—she is only fifteen—who loved "not wisely but too well." Unlike Mimi she doesn't leave her lover...but *he* leaves *her*—while she waits and waits for his return. It is the tragic, moving story about a girl named Butterfly—whom Puccini loved above all his heroines.

"There is no comparison between my love for Mimi, Musetta, Manon and Tosca and that love which I have in my heart for her whom I wrote music in the night." For Puccini did awake night after night to quickly write down the musical ideas that were to become one of the most popular operas in the world.

From Paris, then, let's travel over the seas to far off Japan! But, strangely enough we will get there by way of (believe it or not) York, Pennsylvania! It is from here that a young man's little story found its way to *Century Magazine,* published in January of 1898. John Luther Long, born during America's Civil

War in 1861, lived to be sixty-six years old. Little is known about the shy young lawyer who didn't even want to send in the story. (In fact, it was a close friend who actually mailed it in.) But he left a treasure that is with us to this day...and that will stay with us forever.

Soon the brilliant American playright, David Belasco, had made the story into a one act play. And it was in London, during the summer of 1900, that Puccini paid a visit to the Duke of York's Theatre and saw the play. Although he hardly understood a word of English, the composer instantly realized the wonderful possibilities of little Cio-Cio-San (Cho-Cho-Sahn).

The moment he returned to Italy he asked his publisher, Ricordi, to get the rights to the play. He wanted above all to start his librettists, Giacosa and Illica, thinking about the innocent geisha who was child and woman, wife and mother...and who blindly loved an American seaman who was unworthy of her.

And so into the world of music was born a delicate spirit— timid, yet with an inner strength—a beautiful young girl—the child bride—who will forever be known as...

8

Madama Butterfly

Lucky for us that fate did not take away her creator before this lovely youngster came to life. Puccini was finally happy with what he had written. And his librettists had finally agreed on everything and the composer was sure his sweetheart *Butterfly* was going to be a great success.

However, on February 25, 1903 he and his wife and son were driven by their young chauffeur, Guido Barsuglia, to Lucca. Here Puccini was to be examined for his constant throat ailment. Everything went well until the trip home.

Then, on a dark and foggy road, the young driver plunged off a sharp curve into a gully below! And, although Elvira and Tonio were spared real injury...the driver and his master were not. In fact, Puccini at first could not be found! He had been thrown from the overturned car and was *under* it...but alive.

Both his legs were badly damaged. He could no longer sit at his piano at Torre del Lago to complete his music. Gradually, however, by summertime, he had recovered enough so that he could be placed in a steel brace.

And so slowly, painfully, with the months rolling by, Puccini at last completed his musical score. It was on December 27, 1903—almost ten months after the near fatal accident (at a little after eleven at night)—that *Madama Butterfly* was completed.

Puccini had brought his little geisha girl to life and was very pleased with her—just as we shall be when we meet her on her wedding day in the first act.

ACT I

Imagine a hilltop overlooking a shimmering harbor. Here and there small boats lie at anchor, or slowly sail by. Imagine, too, a light, airy Japanese house perched on the hill surrounded by fragrant blossoms that perfume the air. It is springtime in the city of Nagasaki, sometime in the late 1800's.

It is also the day that the young United States Navy Lieutenant, Benjamin Franklin Pinkerton, is to marry a Japanese girl who has caught his eye. At the moment, he is being shown how the house "works"...with all its sliding panels...by his marriage arranger and house salesman, Goro.

The busy sound of violins introduces the scene. Pinkerton is surprised at how the walls—and even the ceilings—move so easily! When they get back to the garden, Goro claps his hands and three servants appear. One of them is Suzuki, the chambermaid and Butterfly's close friend. The music is slow and soft. Suzuki begins chattering about how nice it is to smile as she sees Pinkerton looking pleased.

> "The wise Ocunama said a smile tears away a web of trouble...."

But soon Goro, afraid that all this talk might annoy his good customer, claps his hands and the servants quickly disappear.

"What are you looking at?" asks Pinkerton.

"To see if your bride is finally coming."

Pinkerton is very happy with his "gem" of an agent. He wonders if there will be a lot of relatives and in a perky little tune Goro spells out who will soon be arriving.

"Her mother...her grandmother, an uncle who is a priest (and will not come)...and all the cousins...."

Then he mentions slyly that for descendents Pinkerton will have to depend on himself "and the beautiful Butterfly."

"What a pearl of an agent!"

Just as he says this we hear a voice huffing and puffing and complaining about the steep hill. It is the American Consul, Sharpless.

"Oof!"

"Quick, Goro, get something to drink...."

"That's steep," comments Sharpless.

"But beautiful!" beams Pinkerton.

Yes, the sea and the harbor of Nagasaki is really lovely, admits the consul. And, proudly pointing to the little house, Pinkerton explains that it does anything he wants it to do. He bought it for nine hundred and ninety-nine years—but he can cancel the contracts (house *and* marriage) *anytime!*

We hear the strains of the "Star Spangled Banner." (Puccini not only flavored the music with the national anthem but also with bits of Japanese-sounding melodies that do so much to bring color to the story.) The lieutenant now sings an aria that shows us what kind of a person he really is: The young, devil-may-care sailor who has a girl in every port... "dropping anchor wherever he pleases...."

Sharpless is polite but doesn't much like this thinking. He knows that it can lead to trouble.

"It's an easy belief. . . that might make life wonderful—but can sadden the heart. . . ."

Sharpless, wiser and older, can see the possible tragedy. He tries to warn Pinkerton as best he can—but gets nowhere.

". . .and that's the way I'm getting married—Japanese style—for nine hundred and ninety-nine years. . .and I can get out of it every month!"

Once again Sharpless notes that it is "an easy belief." But, to the sound of horns playing the anthem, Pinkerton gets up and offers a toast. They touch glasses and drink a rousing salute to "America forever!"

When they sit again Sharpless asks if the girl is pretty. Well, Goro, looking for another customer, steps in to say that she's just like "a garland of fresh flowers!" Wouldn't the consul himself like one from a big selection at. . . "only a hundred yen?" Sharpless laughs this off while Pinkerton—impatient—tells Goro to go get his future bride. Goro rushes off down the hill.

Again Sharpless, still worried, wonders if Pinkerton really knows what he's doing.

"What kind of passion has taken hold of you? Are you wholly captured. . .?"

In a restless aria Pinkerton admits he doesn't know whether he's really in love or if it's just a passing fancy. All he knows is that Butterfly has put a spell on him. . . "fragile as a thin glass". . . the way she stands, the way she walks. . . she's like a "figure on a painted screen."

Then ending on a high note he declares that he's forced to run after her. . . "even though I hurt her wings."

Sharpless still thinks that this whole thing may not be such a good idea. Only the other day, when the girl was in his office—even though he did not see her—he heard her speak. He was touched by the mysterious charm of her voice.

"Truly, only a sincere love speaks like that. . . ."

And it would be a very bad thing to "strip off those delicate wings" and perhaps break that trusting heart.

It's no use. Though Pinkerton tells Sharpless not to worry, the consul still frets about the poor girl's fate. A "divine...sweet-voiced" girl like that should not be made to suffer pain.

This goes in one ear and out the other! Instead Pinkerton offers him more whiskey. He drinks to the consul's family far away and to the day when he'll have a *real* wedding with a *real* American bride! Before Sharpless can answer this the light, melodious voices of Butterfly and her girl friends are heard in the distance. They admire the wonderful view.

"Ah...there's so much sky! So much sea!"

"One more step and we'll be there," sings Butterfly.

Butterfly is the happiest girl in Japan. She is deeply in love. Her friends wish her well again and again. Finally, they all arrive. All are beautifully gowned and are carrying light, colorful parasols. On a thrilling high note Butterfly sings..."we are here!!"

She then quickly closes her parasol as she instantly sees her future husband. She points him out to her friends and announces, "F.B. Pinkerton." (Of course, it's really the other way around—B.F.—but Puccini quickly shows us the little girl in Butterfly, one who may not be ready for this serious giant step.)

"Wasn't the climb a little hard?" asks Pinkerton.

"To a ready bride, being impatient is even more painful!"

Pinkerton is pleased at this "rare compliment." But when Butterfly offers to show off some more, he tells her "no, thank you."

Sharpless is fascinated by all the girls, all the color. He tells the bride-to-be that she is well named. Does she come from Nagasaki? Oh, yes, and at one time her family was quite wealthy. She turns to her friends.

"Isn't that true?"

"It's true!"

But things did not turn out well for them so they became geishas to make a living.

"True?"

"True!"

And so the small talk goes on. Pinkerton is in "flames" over the child-like Butterfly. Sharpless finds out that she does have a mother, but her father is dead. All bow their heads. Goro gets nervous. Sharpless wants to know her age. In a coy little voice Butterfly asks him to guess.

"Ten."

"Go up...."

"Twenty."

"Come down...Just exactly fifteen; I'm already old!"

Of course, Sharpless is amazed. He can't get over how young she is. Butterfly should really be out playing games...instead.

Goro announces, with great importance, that the Imperial Commissioner, and the Official Registrar—along with all the relatives—have arrived!

Pinkerton *still* doesn't take things seriously. He believes the whole thing is a farce, especially all these relatives that he has "hired" by the month. Butterfly, innocently, is busy showing off her love. A jealous cousin comments that he's really not handsome. Butterfly tells her that he's so handsome—no one could be more good-looking!

"To me he looks like a king!" cries her mother.

Goro had offered him to *her,* insists this cousin, but she refused him! This doesn't bother Butterfly in the least since she doesn't believe a word of it.

And so the chitter-chatter goes on. Gossip and more gossip. Some say that Butterfly is already becoming a snob. Some that she's already losing her looks. Where's the wine? Isn't there

any wine? Pinkerton is worth a fortune. That cousin is still saying that she once told Goro that she didn't want Pinkerton.
Sharpless thinks Pinkerton is a very lucky man. The groom is
overcome by Butterfly's beauty and exotic perfume!

"Yes, she truly is a flower...a flower!"

On and on the voices mingle in a swirl of typical gossip. Finally, at a sign from Butterfly, they all bow before Sharpless and
Pinkerton. And slowly they begin to wander around the garden.
Some go inside. We hear the strains of the love theme. Pinkerton
now has a chance to take Butterfly by the hand to show her the
house. But—still calling him Mister F.B. Pinkerton—she
apologizes for taking along some "feminine objects." And where
does she have them? In her sleeves! Out come handkerchiefs,
a sash, a mirror, a fan, a jar of rouge...Then she takes out a
long, narrow case. What could it be? She can't show what's inside because there are "too many people." She quickly takes
it indoors. But we soon find out from Goro that it is the knife
by which her father committed suicide at the command of the
Mikado! When Butterfly returns she shows Pinkerton some little statues. They are the spirits of her ancestors. In a fearful
aria, Butterfly explains that yesterday she secretly went to the
mission alone. Well, since she is to begin a new life, she should
also adopt a new religion. No one knows about this. Especially
not her uncle, the priest! It is her fate...her destiny...to fall
in love with Mister Pinkerton. So she will follow her destiny,
pray to *his* God and kneel in the same church. And in making
him happy, maybe she will be able to forget about her own people. She ends her little story on a soaring high note...while the
orchestra's deep tones remind us of the sorrow that Butterfly
may one day feel.

"Quiet everybody!" calls Goro.

The ceremony is about to begin. The commissioner announces
that Benjamin Franklin Pinkerton, Lieutenant on the warship,
Lincoln, United States Navy (North America) and Miss Butterfly
from the Omara district of Nagasaki are allowed to be married—

first because they want to, and then because her relatives agree! And without any further rites he asks them to sign the deed! Goro shows them where.

First the bridegroom. . .then the bride. And it's all over. Everyone crowds around the newlyweds.

"Madama Butterfly!"

"Madama F.B. Pinkerton," corrects Butterfly proudly.

"Many good wishes," says the commissioner to Pinkerton.

"My thanks. . . ."

The official asks Sharpless if he is now leaving. Not having any success with the new husband, Sharpless decides to go and tells Pinkerton that he will see him tomorrow. And then, before he finally leaves, the consul—to sorrowful music—gives him a knowing look and warns him to be sensible. Pinkerton just waves goodbye.

He's now a married man! He wants to hurry and get rid of everybody so he can be alone with his bride. He offers a toast. They drink to a lilting, swaying melody.

"O Kami! O Kami! Let's all drink to the new union. . . ."

Suddenly, from a distance, there's the sound of a deep and threatening voice. It's Butterfly's uncle—The Bonze!

"Cio-Cio-San! Cio-Cio-San! Curses upon you!"

Her uncle the priest! All are terribly frightened. They all shy away from poor Butterfly.

There he is! The fearful Buddhist priest—followed by two others. Pointing an accusing finger at the shaking girl he cries, "What did you do at the mission?"

And with her jealous cousin leading the rest, they call on her to answer! Pinkerton is angry at this interruption.

"What's that crazy one screaming about?"

"Answer Cio-Cio-San!" insists The Bonze.

But Butterfly is too overcome with fear. And when her uncle tells them that she has renounced her religion...has renounced them all...they are stunned!

"Hou! Cio-Cio-San!"

By now Pinkerton has had enough. And that's what he tells the priest. Enough! Enough!

The Bonze orders everyone to leave with him.

"...You have renounced us...so we will renounce you!"

Everyone rushes to the path leading down the hill. Butterfly's mother tries to go to her but she, too, is swept away. The voices cry over and over again that they are rejecting her!

Slowly they die away. The light is fading. It is becoming night. Faintly another cry is heard far away...as Butterfly, with her hands covering her face...bursts into tears.

"Baby, baby, don't cry at the croaking of a few frogs."

"They're still screaming at me!"

With great tenderness, Pinkerton tries to comfort the unhappy young girl. All her "tribe" and all the priests in Japan aren't worth the tears from those beautiful eyes. With little-girl hope Butterfly looks up and asks if that is true. Well, then, she won't cry anymore. She tries to kiss his hand...as Pinkerton wonders what she is doing. Butterfly has heard that among ladies and gentlemen kissing the hands shows great respect!

They're suddenly interrupted by a voice from inside the house. We hear a lot about the god, "Kami." With a little laugh Butterfly explains that it is only Suzuki saying her evening prayers.

And now to the stirring music of the violins the fantastic love duet of the opera begins. Puccini pulled out all the stops to give us music full of passion, innocence and beauty.

"Comes the night," sings Pinkerton.

"...and the shadows and the silence," murmurs Butterfly.

Then in a sweet voice she remembers that she is indeed all

alone—banished but happy. Suzuki will prepare her night clothes, and with her help she dresses in a pure white gown. She leaves her mistress sitting on a cushion doing her hair. Pinkerton can't get over how graceful, how delicate she is. Butterfly in turn is very much aware of his admiring glances. She blushes...yet the angry voices are still in the back of her mind. As she steps once again onto the terrace, Pinkerton holds out his arms to her.

"Child...with eyes so full of witchery, now you are all mine...."

He is enchanted that she is all in white like a lovely lily. And he likes her dark hair against the white of her veil. Butterfly is full of joy.

"I am like...the little Goddess of the Moon who comes down at night from...heaven...."

But, he complains, she hasn't yet told him that she loves him. Does this goddess know those words? Yes, she does but she wonders if she would die on hearing them! Pinkerton assures her that love does not kill...but gives life, and smiles with joy as it is doing now in her oval eyes.

They are very close now. Pinkerton caresses her. Suddenly, Butterfly draws away. She has liked him from the moment she saw him—he is so tall and strong...and he says things that she has never heard before. And so she is truly happy. She looks at him timidly, then slowly goes to him again where he is sitting on a garden bench. She kneels at his feet and looks up at him tenderly with pleading eyes. In a child-like voice she asks him to "love her," to give her the kind of love that he would have for a small child.

"We are people used to little things...to a flowery tenderness...and yet one that is as high as the sky and as deep as the sea!"

Pinkerton takes her hands..."and let me kiss them."

"My Butterfly! How well they have named you...."

But Butterfly wonders a bit fearfully at the stories about captured butterflies that are stuck to a table with pins! Pinkerton admits that there is some truth to that but it is done so that they will not fly away. He lovingly folds her in his arms.

"I have caught you...you are mine!"

"Yes, for life..."

He begs her to come with him...to banish her fears on this clear night where all is asleep. Butterfly looks up at the sky. She draws back from him once again. Pinkerton still insists that she come with him. But she is amazed by the number of stars. She has never seen so many! Never so beautiful! Now fireflies flit about them both, flickering among the flowers and bushes. To Butterfly they are as so many eyes...peering from all sides.

Pinkerton takes her in his arms and leads her toward the cottage and, as their voices climb gloriously, we hear Butterfly sing about how the sky itself is smiling!

"Ah! Sweet night! Everything is ecstatic with love...."

"Come with me! You are mine!"

The music plays softly to their steps as they disappear through the filmy doorway...while the curtain falls.

ACT II

We are in a room in the little hilltop house. Three long years have gone by. Pinkerton left her so long ago, but Butterfly—now eighteen—has never lost hope, though she has shed many tears.

Suzuki is saying her prayers to Buddha. She, too, has suffered with her unhappy mistress. Please, oh gods, don't let Butterfly cry anymore! We hear a soulful flute, with bass strings joining in. The prayer bell rings. There is a steady sad beat to the music. Butterfly raises her head from her hands and cries out.

"The Japanese gods are fat and lazy!"

She's sure that the western God is quicker to answer those who beg him...but he probably doesn't know where they live! The gentle sound of the oboe tells us of this young woman's deep suffering.

How long will it be before they run out of money? Suzuki shows her a few coins. If Pinkerton doesn't return soon, they will be desperate. Butterfly can't bear the thought. She stands and turns to her faithful friend.

"But he *will* come back...."

The violins play in sympathy. Once again, with greater force, she cries that he *will come back!* Now she has to take her sadness out on somebody, and Suzuki is the only one there.

"Why does he have the consul keep on paying the rent? Well, answer that! And why did he have locks put on all the doors...if he wasn't coming back again?"

"I don't know."

Well, Butterfly will tell her! To keep out mosquitoes, relatives and problems! While inside, jealously guarded, is Butterfly—his bride. We begin to hear the wonderful theme that she will soon be singing.

But Suzuki doesn't seem to know any better and before she can hold back she says the one thing that will make Butterfly furious. No one has ever heard of a foreign husband coming back to his "nest!" Butterfly has dreaded this thought for three years. Now it was out!

"Ah! Shut up...or I'll kill you!"

She tries to help herself. On that final morning she had asked him if he would come back. He, with a heavy heart, to calm her fears, answered with a smile. (As she speaks the music recalls the first time he made love to her.) She knows word for word the last things he said to her.

"Oh, Butterfly, tiny little wife, I will return with the roses in that peaceful season when the robin makes his nest."

Then with greater firmness, because she wants to believe this
so badly, she once again insists that he *will* return! She demands
that Suzuki repeat with her that he will return. Suzuki
obeys...then cannot hold back her tears. Why is she crying?
Doesn't she have any faith? Well, then, listen.

Now Puccini gives his most-loved heroine an aria that brings
out her very soul. Butterfly has had to grow up very fast during
those painful three years. Yet she has not lost her little-girl ability
to make believe. And while Suzuki tearfully listens and watches,
Butterfly gently, softly, as if in a dream, begins her hopeful song.

> "One fine day...we will see rising a thread of smoke...out
> there on the horizon of the sea. And then the ship will ap-
> pear...then the white ship will enter the harbor...."

Butterfly can see this all happening. She starts to act out her
imagination. A cannon from the ship roars its salute! (The kettle drum of the orchestra thunders.) There, you see? He has
come! She will not go down to meet him. Oh, no, not her. She'll
stand on the rim of the hill and wait...wait a long time—and
it will not tire her to wait.

Then—out of the civilian crowd—steps a man! Just a tiny
speck...starting to climb the hill! Well, who can it be? And when
he gets here, what will he say? Butterfly knows. Her voice colors
lovingly.

> "He will call 'Butterfly'...from far away...."

And she, without answering, will stay hidden. (Now the small
girl and the grown woman blend together.) Why will she stay
hidden? First, to play a little joke—and then, so that she will not
die (her voice soars) at this first meeting! And then, and
then...he will call to her—call to her...

> "Tiny little wife...fragrant as verbena..."

It is what he had called her when first they met! She turns
to Suzuki and points her finger at her. All this will happen, she
promises. "You can keep your fears," she sings, "while I, with
full faith—will wait for him!" Her voice ends on a desperate but

beautiful high note...as the orchestra repeats the melody with which she began. With a small sign, she sadly lets Suzuki go.

Suddenly Goro and, more importantly, Sharpless arrive. After a knock on the door, the consul comes in. Butterfly has her back to him.

"Excuse me...Madama Butterfly..."

Butterfly doesn't yet know who it is but she does know that she is Madama Pinkerton, if you please! But when she turns and sees her visitor she can't help giving a cry of delight.

We can imagine what must be going through her mind. Maybe at last this will be the beginning of the end of her long wait. After all she is really an American, in an American home. She must act the part—a young grownup lady who is the wife of an American officer. (She must also keep from turning into the anxious child that her emotions are trying to make her.) With great charm and grace she politely asks him about his grandparents and ancestors! Would he like a smoke?

Well, all this small talk just makes Sharpless more nervous than ever. He has an important letter from Pinkerton and he's trying to get Butterfly to listen to it. Although she doesn't know about the letter, could it be that she suspects something? If so, she secretly must dread it, while still hoping it is good news. Against all her instincts she tries to play it cool!

"Benjamin Franklin Pinkerton has written to me..."

"Really? Is he in good health?"

"Perfectly."

The music takes on a Japanese flavor. Butterfly is the happiest woman in Japan! She hurries on to ask the question that has been on her mind for three years. Out of the clear, blue sky she wants to know when the robins nest in America. Sharpless is startled.

"What was that?"

"Yes, before or after they do here?"

The consul is baffled. (In the back Goro is listening.) Butterfly patiently explains that her husband told her that he would return when the robins nested...and here they have already nested three times! So?

At this Goro can't help laughing. Butterfly is annoyed, but what can you expect from a marriage broker? She tells him to shut up. And with a bow, Goro goes back into the garden.

Now let's get on with it. What about the robins? Sharpless doesn't really know how to get out of this. All he can think of is to say he doesn't know ornithology (the study of birds). This is an awfully big word!

"Orni...," tries Butterfly

"...thology," completes Sharpless.

That means he doesn't know decides Butterfly. Once again Sharpless tries to read her the letter. Meanwhile, Puccini's music is painting us a picture full of Butterfly's many emotions. She's terribly lonely...and proud, happy, angry and filled with hope. And afraid! She can't take the chance of having him read that letter. So she chatters on about how Goro has been trying to get her to marry a rich Japanese named Yamadori. (The music again takes on a Japanese tone.)

Sure enough there is Yamadori, with Goro, paying Butterfly another visit! Well, she'll have none of him! She teases him about all his other wives (even though he promises to let them all go if she would marry him). Goro, trying to make another sale, explains that Yamadori has villas, servants, gold, a palace. But it's no use. Butterfly is already married.

"She believes she's still married...."

"I don't just believe...I *am*, I *am*."

But the law says that if a wife is deserted then she's divorced!

"The Japanese law...not the law of *my* country."

"Which one?" wonders Goro.

"The United States!"

Well, now Sharpless is truly unhappy. He feels for Butterfly. He can see that she is becoming a mature woman right before his eyes. He has to agree with her that you can't get a divorce so easily in America. Proudly, she turns to the other two. There in America a knowing judge throws a husband in jail for trying to leave his wife! She calls for tea.

Now, privately, the three men talk about the situation. Sharpless is very unhappy about her "blindness." Goro knows that Pinkerton's ship is about to arrive. Yamadori sighs at the thought of when she sees Pinkerton again. And that's the trouble. The consul whispers that Pinkerton doesn't *want* to meet her...and he, Sharpless, had come up to help her know the real story! He stops short, Butterfly is coming with the tea. Soon Yamadori and Goro get up to leave. (They can't get anywhere anyhow.) The music plays the same flowing melody with which Butterfly greeted her Japanese hopeful.

"And now for us...will you sit here and read me this letter?"

But before Sharpless can say a word, Butterfly takes the letter, kisses it and hugs it to her. Then returning it, she settles down to hear what it says.

"My friend, find that lovely flower of a girl..."

Butterfly can't stand it. She's bursting with hope.

"Is that really what it says!?"

Sharpless assures her that it's true, but he complains that if she is going to interrupt all the time...

Butterfly promises not to stop him again. He starts in once more. (Sharpless, in a very real way, is the real "hero." He's the one that has to try to break the sorry news to Butterfly. He's the one who shows us how important it is to know a person's helplessness and need for sympathy. He is a good, understanding and truthful man.)

"Since that happy time, three years have passed..."

Butterfly can't help it.

"He has counted them too!"

"And perhaps Butterfly doesn't remember me anymore."

Well, this is more than she can stand! Not remember him? The thought is laughable! She turns to Suzuki to prove how very much she *does* remember him. Sharpless, trying bravely to carry on, whispers to himself that he must have patience.

"If she still loves me, if she is waiting for me..."

This, then, is too much for Butterfly! She grabs the letter from him...

"Oh, sweet words! You wonderful thing!" she says as she kisses the letter again.

Sharpless is filled with emotion. Gently he takes back the letter to try to get to the awful part. Pinkerton is going to ask him to break the news to Butterfly that he will not come back to her. But Sharpless never gets that far.

Butterfly is now sure "he is coming!" Suzuki knows better. Love has made her mistress blind. Too excited to listen she only wants to know how soon Pinkerton will arrive! And the consul, knowing that it is useless to go on, quietly puts the letter back into his pocket.

He gets up. (That devil Pinkerton!) He must try again. Turning to the happy girl he asks, with a heavy heart, what she would do if Pinkerton were never to return! Butterfly is stunned! The orchestra thunders. Trying hard to get the words out she tells him she could do two things: go back to being a geisha—or better yet, *die*.

Sharpless tenderly takes her hand. He is suffering along with this child-bride. Accept Yamadori, he advises. The music, with sweeping sadness, follows Butterfly's sobbing as she wonders aloud....

"You...you sir, tell me this! You?"

She suddenly wants Sharpless to leave...but then regrets what she has said and asks him to stay. He has hurt her very much...so very much! She seems about to faint but catches herself..."it passes like the clouds over the sea." Then, unable to hold it in any longer, she cries out—her voice reaching the sky—*"Ah! He has forgotten me!"*

She rushes from the room only to return just as quickly. In her arms is a beautiful, blond, curly-headed child! The music crashes, the horns blare as she holds out the little boy...

"And this one? And this one? Will he also be able to forget this one too?" she cries desperately.

Sharpless, a father himself, cannot believe his eyes. This boy is Pinkerton's? Well, what Japanese child has blue eyes...and such golden curls? No, Pinkerton does not know. So tell him, tell him...and he will quickly come back to her and his child that was born when he was away in his big country.

In a pitiful aria she asks the little one if he knows what this gentleman had the heart to believe? That she would beg in the streets to get enough food to feed themselves, that she would go back to being a geisha and with a trembling hand ask people for charity! Violins accompany her as she falls to her knees. No, no...she would never go back to that! Better that she should die. No, she will never dance like that...she would rather put an end to her life!

"Ah! Death!" she sobs, her voice climbing, as the music plays Japanese-flavored chords.

By now Sharpless can no longer hold back his own tears. Butterfly takes hold of herself and prepares to bid farewell to the deeply affected consul. She holds out her child's hands. Sharpless takes them warmly. He can't get over the boy's lovely blond hair. And his name? Today, Butterfly tells him, the child's name is "Sorrow." But if the consul will write and tell "Daddy"...then the day he comes back to them—his name will be "Joy!" Her voice is now high and beautiful. The music brings in the theme of the moving aria Butterfly will soon sing. With great emotion, Sharpless promises the boy that his father will surely know about him. He quickly leaves.

> *(For reasons unknown, some who should know bet-ter make the mistake of calling Butterfly's son "Trouble." She tells Sharpless that the boy's name is* Dolore, *which translates as "Sorrow." But if his father comes to her, then the name will be* Gioia, *"Joy." Obviously, one doesn't go from "trouble" to "joy" but from "sorrow" to "joy".)*

Outside there's shouting! Suzuki has discovered Goro lurk-ing about and is dragging him inside the house. Goro had the nerve to gossip that no one really knows who the father is! He even said that in America when a "cursed" child is born everybody rejects him!

"You lie!" screams the furious Butterfly.

Now she has her father's dagger.

"Say that again and I'll kill you!"

Suzuki stops her. Butterfly pushes the terrified Goro away. Then she returns the knife to its shrine. She assures her little boy that one day his father will come and take them far away...far away...She is deep in her hopeful thoughts. Sud-denly, the dull thud of a cannon is heard! Then silence. Can it be at last?

It's the port cannon announcing the arrival of a ship! A *war-ship!* It's white...white...flying the star-spangled banner! (The music plays a few notes of the anthem.) Butterfly runs for binoculars. The name. The name! There it is: *Abraham Lincoln!*

"They were all lying!" cries Butterfly.

"All!! Only I knew it...only I who love him," she sings high into the heavens.

Now see how foolish Suzuki was to doubt? Just when everyone

was telling us to cry and doubt.

"My love is triumphant," she sings to the melody of America's anthem.

"He has come back and he loves me!"

And with her voice soaring, with the orchestra joining her in final victory, Butterfly runs joyfully out on the terrace. She wants to cover her feverish face with cherry blossoms. She doesn't know what to do next. How long will it be before he climbs the hill to her? An hour? More than that. Maybe two hours. The whole house must be full of flowers. Let's do it right now. Let's get the peach blossoms...the violets, jasmine. Even if the whole garden turns into a desert!

And so Suzuki does as she is told. She comes in with her arms full of flowers. But Butterfly wants even more. She wants springtime in the house. Scatter lilies, roses everywhere... petals of all kinds of flowers.

Now their voices blend in a gorgeous melody that carries them along as the flowers are drifted around. It sways and floats as the two happy women prepare for the grand homecoming.

Finally, Butterfly decides to get herself ready. She sits at her dressing table, but asks Suzuki to first bring her the child. She sadly looks at herself in a small hand mirror. (Remember Violetta, from *La Traviata,* saying how pale she looked when she saw herself in the mirror?)

"I am not the same girl anymore! Too many sighs...and these eyes have watched too long into the distance."

She wants a little rouge on her cheeks...and some for the little boy so that the long wait will not make him look pale. While Suzuki is doing her hair Butterfly gloats over what her relatives will say. She laughs at the thought of Yamadori.

The music reminds us of the love duet of the first act. Butterfly wants to be dressed in the same white gown she wore on her wedding night, with a red poppy in her hair.

Everyone's ready. Now is the time for waiting. She carefully slides the door closed overlooking the harbor. Then she punches three tiny holes in the screen so that each of them can see without being seen!

"...and we'll be as quiet as mice, and we'll wait...."

Here we have one of the most touching, most dramatically beautiful scenes in opera, the waiting scene. (On stage, in the Belasco original, without a word being spoken, this night vigil lasted a full fourteen minutes! The audience was completely overcome—as was Puccini—as the night grew darker, the stars slowly appeared...and the lanterns gradually died out, one after the other.)

And on *our* stage, now, we see the three lonely figures, dark against the moonlit wall. The boy has fallen asleep. Even the faithful Suzuki has dropped off. Only Butterfly is awake, dreaming, hoping, loving. Far off—as if from the star-filled sky—a sorrowful humming of female voices rises and falls...a humming of a sweet melody that at last swells and rises ever higher as it gradually comes to a peaceful end. The curtain carefully closes on this most heart-breaking musical and dramatic experience.

ACT III

With a crashing fanfare the mood is set for the end of poor Butterfly. The kettle drums rumble. Little melodies we've heard before enter and leave. Then a flowing theme begins—full of sadness, beauty and hope. The voices of harbor men starting for work are heard.

There are the three hopefuls. By now it is daybreak. The light slowly becomes brighter. There is repeated thudding of the drums...and then, finally, the love theme breaks through...only to gradually come to a soft close.

Only Butterfly is still awake, her small figure so pitiful against the growing glare of day. The cheerful chirping of birds greet a new beginning. The music takes on an Oriental tone. It grows more excited and then bursts out as the fullness of the day arrives. But soon it fades away with the violins climbing sweetly higher and higher as Suzuki suddenly awakens.

A new musical theme is played.

"Already the sunshine!" cries Suzuki.

And although Butterfly is still awake, she seems to be in a dream. Suzuki shakes her gently as she calls her name. But all that Butterfly can say is...

"He will come, he *will* come, you'll see...."

She picks up the still sleeping child and begins to carry him to bed. Suzuki wants her to rest too, assuring her that she will call her the moment Pinkerton arrives.

From the next room we hear Butterfly singing a soft lullaby.

"Sleep, my love...sleep upon my heart. You are with God...while I am with my pain...my baby...sleep!"

Her voice reaches the heavens, while Suzuki repeats the refrain..."Poor Butterfly."

Someone knocks at the door! Suzuki slides away the panel and is shocked to see both Sharpless—and Pinkerton! She gives a cry.

"Sssssh! Quiet! Don't disturb her!" warns Pinkerton.

Suzuki explains that the tired Butterfly waited for him all night long...with her child. How did she know? For three long years there wasn't a ship that she didn't see, always watching and waiting for the right flag.

Sharpless had told Pinkerton to be careful from the very beginning. See? Last night all these flowers were placed everywhere in the room. Again Sharpless reminds him.

"Didn't I tell you?"

Now, at last, Pinkerton begins to know what he has done. He begins to feel the pain.

Suddenly Suzuki hears a noise in the garden. It's a woman! Although Pinkerton tries to keep her quiet, she is too excited.

Again and again Suzuki wants to know who it is! And when Pinkerton says lamely that "she came with me"...Sharpless very plainly tells her that it is his wife! Suzuki is overcome. She falls to her knees...her head bows to the floor.

"What's the use...," she cries.

Sharpless, having known all along that this would happen, gently takes her to one side and asks her to help them through this unhappy time.

Here is the start of a lovely melody for all three voices. Sharpless realizes that for Butterfly's deep pain there is nothing that can be done.

"We must think of the baby...."

Pinkerton, no longer that young and selfish boy, looks at the faded flowers. Their bitter perfume seems like poison to his heart. He sadly sees that nothing has changed "in the room of their first love."

Sharpless is trying to convince Suzuki to get Butterfly and the little boy. She can't believe that he wants to ask a mother to give up her child!

There on a table Pinkerton sees his picture. He now understands what he has done. He now knows the long wait, the torture, that the girl has gone through..."counting the days and even the hours!"

The emotional trio comes to an end. Sharpless decides to have Suzuki go into the garden and bring back Kate, Pinkerton's American wife. She leaves in tears.

Now the strain of meeting his child-bride is too much for Pinkerton.

"I can't stay here...Sharpless, I'll wait for you on the path...."

"Didn't I tell you?"

"My sorrow tears me apart...my sorrow tears me apart...."

Again Sharpless reminds him of how he had warned him years ago. He had told him to be careful...that she really believed him. But, although he had been a prophet, Pinkerton had not listened to him. While Butterfly, in the face of all the sneers...all the doubts, had stubbornly waited for him with all her heart.

> "Yes, all of a sudden I can see my folly...and I feel that I shall never get away from this torment! No!"

The bass instruments strike their mournful notes. And over these deep chords Puccini (and his librettists) give Sharpless words that are severe, yet full of sympathy at the same time.

> "Leave...she will receive the sad truth alone."

Pinkerton is now free to go. He has finally grown up...knowing at last how young and foolish he really had been. He takes one last look around...and in a flowing aria bids a final farewell to this "flowery hideaway...." He will always remember that unhappy Butterfly; his pain will always be with him. When Sharpless tells him again of his early warnings, Pinkerton can no longer stand it.

> "I'm running away...running away—I'm vile!"

He quickly takes Sharpless' hand and just as quickly disappears down the hill.

From the edge of the terrace we hear Kate ask Suzuki if she will break the news to Butterfly. She promises to do so.

> "I will treat him as my own son," Kate assures her. Suzuki must be alone with her mistress when she tells her.

> "She will cry so much...she will cry so much!"

Her voice rises at the thought. Kate quietly goes back to the garden. Meanwhile Butterfly must have felt something inside her. Suddenly we hear her excited voice. She's calling for her friend. She's not only excited but strangely happy! As she tries to come into the room Suzuki stands in her way...but she bursts past her and begins to look everywhere!

> "He's here, he's here...where's he hiding?"

Then she sees the consul. This just makes her more sure that Pinkerton is somewhere nearby! She's still searching...when there is a sudden quiet. At last it comes to her.

"He isn't here!"

Silence. She sees a strange woman in the garden. Who can she be? And what can she want of her? No one speaks. Suzuki is silently crying. Sharpless is about to say something to this eighteen year old who has just become a fearing child again. Butterfly doesn't want him to say anything! She might drop dead. She turns to Suzuki.

> "You, Suzuki, who are so good, don't cry! And you want only good things for me...answer softly, 'Yes' or 'No'— *is he alive?*"

> "Yes."

The kettle drums roll out their thunder! Butterfly seems as if she is truly struck dead!

> "But he will never come again," says Butterfly quietly.

> "They have told you!"

Butterfly demands an answer!

> "Never again," admits Suzuki.

> "But he did arrive yesterday?"

> "Yes."

There is nothing left. That lady in the garden makes Butterfly afraid. It still has not dawned on her as to who she really is. But when Sharpless tells her that the lady is innocent...is not the reason for her unhappiness, Butterfly suddenly knows! She is his wife!

> "All is dead for me! All is ended! Ah!"

Her voice is high with her pain. Sharpless wants her to have courage. He's no longer able to find the words to comfort her.

> "They want everything from me! My own son!"

There is no more she can do. She must obey "him." Unhappy mother...unhappy mother! Kate is now on the terrace. Can Butterfly forgive her? In a wonderful Puccini melody Butterfly answers that there is no more fortunate woman "under heaven" than "you."

"...don't ever be sad over me...," she asks.

Kate and Sharpless are full of pity for the "poor little thing." And will she let the child go? Butterfly has heard her.

"I can give him the child if he comes looking for him. In half an hour come up the hill again."

As they both leave, Butterfly falls to the ground in tears! Suzuki sadly compares the beat of Butterfly's heart to the beating wings of a captured fly. Butterfly wants the room darkened. She commands Suzuki to close up.

"...outside...there is too much springtime...."

The oboe plays thinly. Where's the boy? Outdoors playing.

"Shall I call him?"

"Let him play. Go keep him company."

The drums rumble. Suzuki suspects what is coming. She begins to cry softly.

"I'll stay with you."

But Butterfly orders her to go. The drums warn us that something terrible is about to happen. She goes to a small shrine and takes down her father's knife.

The drums sound again. She kisses the blade. Then in a level voice she reads what is written on the knife.

"He dies with honor who cannot live with honor!"

Suddenly Suzuki's arm pushes the little boy into the room! She is trying one last time to prevent Butterfly from following that awful tradition. He runs to his mother with open arms. Excited violins follow him.

"You? You? My love, flower of the lily and the rose..."

Then, with her voice climbing higher and higher, she vows that her son will never see his mother die! He will go across the sea and not feel sorrow when he grows up—thinking that his mother deserted him. Then, turning him toward her she asks him to look at her closely, closely...so that he will always remember his mother's face! So that the memory will stay with him—even though faintly—look closely.

"Goodbye, my love! Goodbye, my little love! Go. Play, play."

She sits him down gently and places a small American flag in his hand—and a doll. She lovingly ties a cloth over his eyes. The music threatens. Slowly, carefully she disappears behind the waiting screen. The cymbals clash...as we hear the sound of the knife falling to the floor. The drums rumble, rumble...the horns blare...as Butterfly falls lifeless, reaching for her child.

And then, far off, while the music almost drowns him out, we hear Pinkerton calling too late for the fragile young girl who loved him so very much!

"Butterfly! Butterfly! Butterfly!"

The cymbals clash again and again...while the music—Japanese in style—softly ends. The cymbals beat again...as slowly this tragic, lonely scene comes to a close.

THE CURTAIN FALLS

Although the story of the little geisha girl we have just met was not based on a true person, we know that there have been many "Butterflies" through the years...even to the present day. So real has Cio-Cio-San become that today on a hill in Nagasaki, overlooking the bay, stands a life-size bronze statue of Butterfly gazing forever into the distance while her curly-headed boy is at her feet clinging to her gown.

Puccini was so sure that his newest creation would be a wonderful success that for the first time he invited his family and friends to opening night. But the performance of February 17, 1904 at La Scala, Milan, Italy was a disaster!

It is impossible to know why. To this day no one can really explain what made the audience behave so badly. Laughing, cat-calls, shouts—all were used to destroy the hopes of the composer, the famous impresario Gatti-Gasazza, the writers Luigi Illica and Giuseppe Giacosa, and any others who wanted this latest work to be a big success. Even Italy's star, Rosina Storchio, the first Cio-Cio-San, was booed!

Somebody had put together a gang to ruin Puccini's newest opera. They had been paid and were experienced. Who were these enemies? No one ever found out. But Puccini did not forget. *Butterfly* was never performed again at La Scala for the rest of his life!

The shocked Puccini still had great faith in the girl he had grown to love so much. He went to work to make some changes. Instead of two acts, he made three. Very little music was altered. The already famous Arturo Toscanini would conduct.

Then on May 28, in the much smaller theater of Brescia, not too far from Milan, the second performance of *Madama Butterfly* took place. And it was here that Cio-Cio-San triumphed! The whole superb love duet had to be repeated! The Teatro Grande shook! Thirty-two curtain calls! Seven encores! King Victor Emanuele III himself joined in to praise the composer! And from that moment on *Butterfly* triumphed all over the world...becoming a special favorite of opera-lovers everywhere.

She came to America on October 15, 1906. In Washington, D.C., sung in English, the opera opened at the Columbia Theater (next to Ford's Theater, where President Lincoln had been assassinated). The most expensive seat was just $3.00! But the house would have been sold out even if the top seats had gone for thirty.

The Japanese ambassador, Viscount Aoki, arrived from New York. From there, too, came John Luther Long—the author who gave birth to Cio-Cio-San in 1898! For Butterfly, the American impresario Colonel Henry W. Savage had chosen a beautiful soprano from Budapest—Elsa Szamosy. His Suzuki was a New York girl who was making her American debut—Harriet Behnee. It was a night to remember. All of Washington, it seemed, was there. And all of them made the rafters ring with their applause!

By November 12th the company opened in New York's Garden Theater and played for six weeks! In the audience was the actress who first portrayed Butterfly in Belasco's play—Blanche Bates, along with John Phillip Sousa, the great composer of military marches; and Emma Eames, the legendary Metropolitan Opera star!

Finally, on February 1, 1907 this great new opera held its Metropolitan premier starring the all-time fabulous foursome: Geraldine Farrar, Louise Homer, Enrico Caruso and Antonio Scotti! And to put the frosting on the cake...Giacomo Puccini himself supervised the production!

Through Puccini's wondrous lyrical music and through the love he had for his little star (she is hardly ever off the stage), the delicate Butterfly, though rejected in the opera, has forever found her place in the hearts of millions throughout the world.

And so in this First Volume we have traveled through the Wonderland of Opera visiting villages, cities and lands of all kinds—and meeting people of all kinds: some rich, some poor, many young, others old—all inspired by music and song.

There was the gaiety of Vienna, full of laughter, champagne and waltzes...and the humorous plot of "The Bat"—*Die Fledermaus*. We left for the medieval city of Verona with its hundred year old feud between the Montagues and the Capulets—and the great love of *Romeo and Juliet*. Moving along, we met blustery Dr. Bartolo who wanted Rosina for himself but was fooled by the crafty *Barber of Seville*—Figaro—and the wealthy Count Almaviva.

...And the city of Seville, warm and colorful...but sinister, too, as we discovered when we met the fated gypsy girl *Carmen* and her unhappy lover, Don Jose. (We thrilled to "hear" the song of the bullring.) Then, still in Seville, we saw how *The Force of Destiny*—fate—could shape the future of people despite their will to lead happy, peaceful lives.

Through the magic of music and the stage we entered the world of Violetta, "The Lost One,"—*La Traviata*—and her Paris of wealth and intrigue. But there was another Paris. The one where struggling poets, artists, musicians and philosophers lived their cold Bohemian life, where fun mingled with hunger and love proved fleeting and sad for the girl known as *La Boheme*.

And finally, we met a girl of only fifteen in the exotic city of Nagasaki, Japan, who tried so hard to cling to her only love. The child-bride named *Butterfly* never realized her dream of once again flying into the arms of her beloved.

Now we are back home again, but, like Alice, we'd love to continue our journey, to once again step "through the looking glass" into that other world so full of surprises, dangers, music and fun. We can, you know, just by opening the Second Volume of *The Storybook of Opera!*

APPENDIX

Find the Opera Company Nearest You

UNITED STATES

Alabama
Mobile Opera, Municipal Theatre

Arizona
Arizona Opera Company, Tucson

Arkansas
Arkansas Opera Theatre, Arts Center, Little Rock

California
Opera San Jose, Montgomery Theater
San Diego Opera
San Francisco Opera
Long Beach Opera, Terrace Theater

Colorado
Aspen Music Festival, Aspen
Opera Colorado, Boettcher Hall, Denver

Connecticut
Connecticut Opera, Bushnell Hall, Hartford
Stamford State Opera, Stamford Center

Delaware
Opera Delaware, Grand Opera House, Wilmington

District of Columbia
The Washington Opera, John F. Kennedy Center, Washington, D.C.

Florida
Gold Coast Opera, Omni Auditorium, Pompano Beach
Greater Miami Opera, Dade County Auditorium, Miami
Orlando Opera, Bob Carr Performing Arts Center, Orlando
Palm Beach Opera, West Palm Beach Auditorium
Sarasota Opera, Theater of the Arts, Sarasota
Treasure Coast Opera, St. Lucy Center, Ft. Pierce

Georgia
Augusta Opera, Imperial Theatre

Hawaii
Hawaii Opera Theater, Blaisdell Concert Hall, Honolulu

Illinois
Chicago Opera Theater, Athenaeum Theatre, Chicago

Indiana
Whitewater Opera, Centerville High School Auditorium
Indianapolis Opera, Clowes Memorial Hall

Kentucky
Kentucky Opera, Macauley Theater, Louisville

Maryland
Baltimore Opera, Lyric Opera House

Massachusetts
Boston Lyric Opera, Alumni Auditorium
Opera Company of Boston, Opera House

Michigan
Michigan Opera Theatre, Masonic Temple, Detroit
Opera Grand Rapids, De Vos Hall

Minnesota
Minnesota Opera, St. Paul

Mississippi
Opera South, Mississippi Arts Center

Missouri
Lyric Opera of Kansas City, Lyric Theatre
Opera Theatre of St. Louis

Nebraska
Opera Omaha, Orpheum Theatre

Nevada
Nevada Opera, Pioneer Theater, Reno

New Mexico
Sante Fe Opera

New Jersey
Metro Lyric Opera, Paramount Theater, Asbury Park

Opera Classics of New Jersey, De Nooyer Auditorium, Hackensack
New Jersey State Opera, Symphony Hall, Newark

New York
Caramoor Festival, Katonah
Chautauqua Opera, Chautauqua
Lake George Opera Festival, Glens Falls
Metropolitan Opera House, Lincoln Center
National Grand Opera, Tilles Center, C. W. Post Campus, L. I.
New York City Opera, NY State Theatre, Lincoln Center
Opera Theatre of Rochester
Syracuse Opera, Crouse-Hinds Concert Theater
Tri-Cities Opera, The Forum, Binghamton

North Carolina
Charlotte Opera, Ovens Auditorium
Piedmont Opera Theater, Stevens Center, Winston-Salem

Ohio
Cincinnati Opera, Music Hall
Cleveland Opera, State Theatre
Opera Columbus, Palace Theatre
Dayton Opera, Memorial Hall
Toledo Opera, Secor Road

Oklahoma
Tulsa Opera, Chapman Music Hall

Oregon
Portland Opera, Civic Auditorium

Pennsylvania
Pennsylvania Opera Theatre, Walnut Street Theatre, Philadelphia
Opera Company of Philadelphia, Academy of Music
Pittsburgh Opera, Heinz Hall

South Carolina
Spoleto Festival USA,

185

Charleston

Tennessee
Chattanooga Opera, Tivoli
Theatre
Knoxville Opera, Tennessee
Theatre
Opera Memphis, Orpheum
Theatre

Texas
Dallas Opera, Majestic
Theater
Houston Grand Opera, Jones
Hall
Fort Worth Opera
San Antonio Grand Opera

Virginia
Virginia Opera, Norfolk
Center Theatre
Wolf Trap Opera, Trap Road,
Vienna

Washington
Seattle Opera, Opera House

Wisconsin
Florentine Opera, Uihlein
Hall, Milwaukee
Madison Opera, Oscar Mayer
Theatre
Skylight Comic Opera, Pabst
Theatre, Milwaukee

INTERNATIONAL

Argentina
Teatro Colon, Buenos Aires

Australia
Australian Opera, Royal
Exchange, N.S.W.

Austria
Salzburger Festspiele,
Salzburg
Staatsoper, Vienna

Belgium
Opera National, (Rue
Leopold), Brussels

Canada
Calgary Opera, Jubilee
Auditorium
Canadian Opera, O'Keefe
Center, Toronto
Edmonton Opera, Jubilee
Auditorium, Alberta
L'Opera De Montreal, Salle
Wilfrid Pelletier
Opera Hamilton, Great Hall,
Ontario
Manitoba Opera, Centennial
Concert Hall
Ottawa Festival Opera,
Confederation Square,

Ontario
Vancouver Opera, Queen
Elizabeth Theatre

Czechoslovakia
National Theatre, Prague

Denmark
Det Kongeliege Teater,
Copenhagen

Finland
Finnish National Opera,
Helsinki

France
Theatre National de l'Opera,
Place de l'Opera, Paris
Opera du Rhin, Strasbourg
Theatre du Capitale,
Toulouse

Germany (East)
Deutsche Staatsoper, Unter
den Linden, Berlin
Komische Opera,
Behrenstrasse, Berlin
Staatsoper Dresden, Dresden
Stadtisches Theater Leipzig,
Leipzig

Germany (West)
Deutsche Oper Berlin, Berlin
Oper der Stadt Koln, Cologne
Opernhaus Frankfurt,
Frankfurt
Hamburgische Staatsoper,
Hamburg
Bayerische Staatsoper,
Munich
Staatstheater am
Gartnerplatz, Munich
Wurttembergisches
Staatstheater, Stuttgart
Festspielleitung Bayreuth,
Bayreuth

Great Britain
Welsh National Opera, John
Street, Wales
Scottish Opera Limited,
Theatre Royal, Scotland
Glyndebourne Festival Opera,
Sussex
English National Opera,
London Coliseum, London
Royal Opera House, Covent
Garden, London

Hungary
Hungarian State Opera
House, Budapest

Israel
Israel National Opera, Tel
Aviv

Italy
Teatro Comunale, Florence
Teatro alla Scala, Milan

Teatro San Carlo, Naples
Teatro dell' Opera Beniamino
Gigli, Rome
Teatro La Fenice, Venice
Arena di Verona, Verona
Festival of Two Worlds,
Spoleto
Teatro Massimo Bellini,
Catania, Sicily
Politeama Garibaldi, Palermo,
Sicily
Teatro Massimo, Palermo,
Sicily

Monaco
Opera de Monte-Carlo,
Casino, Monte Carlo

Netherlands
Nederlandse Operastichting,
Amsterdam

Norway
Den Norske Opera, Oslo

Poland
Teatr Wielki (Grand
Theatre), Warsaw

Portugal
San Carlos Theatre Opera
House, Lisbon

Russia
Kirov Opera and Ballet
Theatre, Leningrad
Bolshoi Opera, Moscow

Spain
Gran Teatro del Liceo,
Barcelona
Royal Opera House, Madrid

Sweden
Royal Opera, Stockholm

Switzerland
Opernhaus Zurich, Zurich
Grand Theatre de Geneve,
Geneve

Venezuela
Opera Metropolitana, Teatro
Municipal, Caracas

Yugoslavia
Slovensko Narodno
Gledalisce, Ljubljana

OPERA TALK

alto (AHL-toe): The lowest female voice. The same as *contralto*.

aria (AH-ree-ah): An air, melody or song, usually sung by one voice.

barcarole (BAR-cah-role): A rollicking, swaying melody.

baritone: A male voice in the lower range, between tenor and bass.

bass (BASE): The lowest male voice.

basso profondo (BAH-so pro-FOHN-doe): A bass voice that can reach below the lowest bass.

baton (bah-TON): The stick the condutor uses.

bel canto (bell-CAHN-toe): It actually means "beautiful singing." A lyrical style, rather than comic or dramatic.

brasses: The instruments in the orchestra made of brass.

brindisi (BREEN-dee-zee): A drinking song; one of the most famous is in *La Traviata*.

buffa (BOOF-ah): As in opera buffa—comic opera style.

buffo (BOOF-oh): An opera comic like Don Bartolo in *The Barber of Seville*.

cabaletta (cah-bah-LET-tah): A fast song, or part, that reminds one of the beating rhythm of a horse's hooves. From the Spanish *caballo*, meaning horse.

cavatina (cah-vah-TEE-nah): A simple sweet song as sung by Adina in *The Elixir of Love*.

celeste: A musical instrument that gives bell-like tones.

chest tones: Singing tones that come from the chest.

chord: A group of three or more notes played together.

chorus: A group of people who sing all together.

claque (clack): A group of people hired to applaud.

coloratura (cuh-loh-rah-TOOR-ah): A singer, usually female, who sings colorful, flighty, trilling (and thrilling) notes. Violetta in *La Traviata*.

contralto (cohn-TRAHL-toe): The lowest female voice.

crescendo (creh-SHEN-doe): Getting louder.

czardas (CHAR-dahsh): A two-piece Hungarian dance, one slow, one fast. Rosalinda sings a czardas in *Die Fledermaus*.

debut (day-BEW): The first time a singer performs.

diction: A singer or actor who pronounces his/her words so that they can be understood clearly, has good diction.

diminuendo (dee-min-u-EN-doe): When the sound gets softer and softer; either a singer or orchestra.

diva (DEE-vah): It actually translates as "goddess." Used to compliment a woman singer.

discord: When notes that are sung or played are out of harmony.

dramatic: A powerful scene; also applies to voices. Dramatic tenor has a heavier quality than a lyric tenor.

duet: When two singers sing together.

encore (AHN-core): Usually when the audience wants a piece done again, or wants an additional song. It's a compliment.

ensemble (ahn-SOM-bell): When voices or instruments come together as a whole.

187

entr'acte (AHN-tract): Between the acts (*Carmen*).

fanfare: An announcement, by sound, that something is about to happen. (Horns, drums, etc.)

finale (fee-NAH-leh): The ending.

fioritura (fee-or-ee-TOO-rah): Flowery singing; a lot of beautiful vocal gymnastics.

flat: When a singer hits a note lower than what it's supposed to be.

forte (FOR-tay): Strong, loud.

fortissimo (for-TEES-seemo): Very loudly.

head tones: Singing tones that come from the head.

heldentenor: A strong male voice with trumpet-like top notes and baritone low notes. Usually needed in German operas.

impresario: A manager of an opera company.

intermezzo (in-tehr-METZ-oh): A musical piece usually played between two acts.

legato (leh-GAH-toe): A smooth connection of notes.

leitmotif (LITE-moh-teef): A musical reminder about a character or plot.

librettist (li-BRET-tist): The writer of the words used in an opera.

libretto: The booklet that has the words of an opera.

lyric: A light quality of voice. Also the words of a piece.

lyric bass: A light, rather than a strong, dramatic bass voice.

lyric soprano: A light, rather than a strong, dramatic soprano voice; Adele in *Fledermaus*.

lyric tenor: A light, rather than a strong, dramatic tenor voice. Count Almaviva in *The Barber of Seville*.

madrigal (MAD-ree-gahl): A lyrical love poem.

mezzo-soprano: A female voice lower than a soprano, higher than a contralto.

octave: From one note to eight notes later.

operetta: A light, rather than a grand opera.

orchestration: The way a composer writes down notes for the instruments of the orchestra.

overture: The piece of music that's played before the curtain goes up.

pants role: A part played by a woman dressed as a man. (Prince Orlofsky in *Fledermaus*)

percussion: The instruments that include drums, cymbals, etc.

piano: To play softly; pianissimo, very softly.

pitch: The level of a certain sound. To be "off-pitch" means the sound or tone of the voice (or instrument) is off.

pizzicato (peetz-ee-CAH-toe): Plucking the strings instead of bowing them.

portamento (por-tah-MEN-toe): When a note is carried over to the next line of singing.

prelude: A musical piece that sets the mood for what is to come. The prelude to the third act of *La Traviata*.

premiere: An opera's first performance.

prima donna: A female singer who is a star; actually means "first lady." Sometimes it refers to a singer who is hard to get along with.

prologue: The part that's performed before the opera really starts; it explains things ahead of time, as in

Romeo et Juliette. (Not every opera has a prologue.)

prompter: The person who feeds the performers their lines so they won't forget. (Unfortunately, he can sometimes be heard too.)

props: The little things that help a scene—books, candles, vases, etc.

proscenium (proe-SEEN-ee-uhm): The arch that frames the stage.

quartet: Four voices singing or four instruments playing. (The famous quartet at the end of *Rigoletto*)

quintet: Five (see quartet).

range: The distance between low notes and high notes that can be reached by a voice.

recitativo (reh-chee-tah-TEE-voh): Words that are more spoken than sung.

refrain: A melody that's sometimes repeated.

repertory: The different operas that a company will perform.

score: The parts that are written for voices and instruments.

septet: Seven (see quartet).

set: The scene where the action takes place.

sextet: Six (see quartet). The famous one is from Donizetti's *Lucia di Lammermoor.*

singspiel (ZING-shpeel): A work with sung as well as spoken words.

solo: Alone.

soprano: Highest female voice.

sotto voce (SOHT-toh VOH-cheh): "Under-voice"; secretive.

spinto: A voice that goes beyond what is expected.

staccato (stah-CAH-toe): Usually rapid, separate notes; opposite of legato.

strings: Violins, violas—instruments played with a bow.

tarantella (tare-an-TELL-lah): A rapid, whirling folk dance.

tempo: The "time" or pace of music.

tenor: Highest male voice.

tessitura (tehs-ee-TOOR-ah): When a piece has a lot of high notes that a singer is required to reach.

transpose: When music is written higher or lower than the original.

tremolo: A "wavering" of the voice that has to be done very carefully.

trill: A "quivering" of the voice between two notes.

trio: Three.

verismo (vehr-EEZ-moe): True-to-life opera.

vibrato (vih-BRAH-toe): A "vibrating" of the voice that needs to be done carefully.

vocalize: When a singer practices.

winds: Instruments that are blown through: oboe, clarinet, brasses etc.

woodwinds: Instruments that may be made of wood or metal: flute, piccolo, bassoon, oboe, clarinet.

SELECT BIBLIOGRAPHY OF COMPOSERS

JOHANN STRAUSS
Fantel, Hans. *The Waltz Kings*. New York:
   Wm. Morrow and Co., 1972.
Jacob, H. E. *Johann Strauss*. New York:
   The Greystone Press, 1940.

CHARLES GOUNOD
Cross, Milton. *Encyclopedia of the Great
   Composers and Their Music*. New York:
   Doubleday and Co., 1953.
*The New Grove Dictionary of Music and
   Musicians*. Vol. 7. New York: St.
   Martin's Press, 1954.

GIOACHINO ROSSINI
Toye, Francis. *Rossini: A Study in
   Tragicomedy*. New York: Alfred A.
   Knopf, 1947.
Toye, Francis. *Rossini*. London: Arthur
   Backer, 1954.
Weinstock, Herbert. *Rossini*. New York:
   Alfred A. Knopf, 1968.

GEORGES BIZET
Cooper, Martin. *Georges Bizet*. London:
   Oxford University Press, 1938.
Curtiss, Mina. *Bizet and His World*. New
   York: Alfred A. Knopf, 1958.
Dean, Winton. *Georges Bizet*. London:
   Cambridge University Press, 1948.

GIUSEPPE VERDI
Baldini, Gabriele. *The Story of Giuseppe
   Verdi*. New York: Cambridge University
   Press, 1980.
Bonavia, Ferruccio. *Verdi*. London: Dobson
   Books, 1947.
de Schauensee, Max. *The Collector's Verdi
   and Puccini*. New York: J. A.
   Lippincott Co., 1978.
Martin, George. *Verdi, His Music, Life and
   Times*. New York: Dodd, Mead and
   Co., 1963.
Shean, Vincent. *Orpheus at Eighty*. New
   York: Random House, 1958.
Toye, Francis. *Giuseppe Verdi, His Life
   and Works*. New York: Alfred A.
   Knopf, 1946.
Walker, Frank. *The Man Verdi*. New York:
   Alfred A. Knopf, 1962.
Ybarra, T. R. *Verdi: Miracle Man of Opera*.
   New York: Harcourt, Brace and Co.,
   1955.

GIACOMO PUCCINI
Greenfeld, Howard. *Puccini*. New York: G.
   P. Putnam and Sons, 1980.
Jackson, Stanley. *Monsieur Butterfly*.
   Briarcliff Manor, New York: Stein and
   Day, Scarborough House, 1974.
Marek, George R. *Puccini: A Biography*.
   New York: Simon and Schuster, 1951.
Mosco and Carner. *Puccini: A Critical
   Biography*. New York: Alfred A. Knopf,
   1959.

GAETANO DONIZETTI
Ashbrook, William. *Donizetti and His
   Operas*. New York: Cambridge
   University Press, 1982.
Weinstock, Herbert. *Gaetano Donizetti*.
   New York: Pantheon Books, 1963.

RICHARD WAGNER
Chancellor, John. *Wagner*. Boston: Little,
   Brown & Co., 1978.
Gal, Hans. *Richard Wagner*. Briar Cliff
   Manor, New York: Stein and Day,
   Scarborough House, 1963.
Gutman, Robert W. *Richard Wagner, the
   Man, His Mind and His Music*. New
   York: Harcourt, Brace and World, Inc.,
   1968.
Gregor-Dellin, Martin. *Richard Wagner,
   His Life, His Work, His Century*. (2nd
   Volume). New York: Harcourt, Brace,
   and Jovanovich, 1983.
Newman, Ernest. *The Life of Richard
   Wagner*. 4 vols. New York: Alfred A.
   Knopf, 1933-1946.

WOLFGANG AMADEUS MOZART
Burk, John N. *Mozart and His Music*. New
   York: Random House, 1959.
Einstein, Alfred. *Mozart: His Character,
   His Work*. New York: Oxford
   University Press, 1945.
Turner, W. J. *Mozart: The Man and His
   Works*. New York: Alfred A. Knopf,
   1938.

ENGLEBERT HUMPERDINCK
*The New Grove Dictionary of Music and
   Musicians*. Vol. 8, 6th ed. Edited by
   Stanley Sadie. New York: Grove
   Dictionaries of Music, Inc., 1980.

PROPER NAME INDEX